Praise for GRANDM

THE

"This is a book that traces a movement that recalls for us the great movement tradition of democracy. It reminds us of the civil rights movement, the suffragette movement, and peace movements of the past, all of which have combined to promote democracy at home and abroad."   —Bill Perkins, New York state senator

"You will love reading *Grandmothers Against the War*. The story about the Grannies—who they are and why they protest—is inspiring and uplifting. It will remind you of the importance of our First Amendment right to peacefully protest, especially these troubled days. And hopefully, it will motivate others to also stand up and speak out."   —Norman Siegel, civil rights attorney

"Walt Whitman abhorred war and injustice, but loved the American people. He wrote, 'I hear America Singing.' He expressed his love for the beauty and majesty of America and its working people. Today he would have paid homage to the Grannies. Joan Wile writes the story of the courage, commitment, and determination of these tribunes of peace as if she is speaking directly to you. For those who have lost hope . . . read the book!"
—Frank J. Barbaro, New York State assemblyman for 24 years; New York State Supreme Court judge

"Ms. Wile's wonderful book must be read by all who despair in the face of the seemingly sisyphean task of putting our country back on the path to peace and justice. It shows that it is possible to stand up to or sit down in front of the powers that be and not only to get their attention but to inspire your fellow citizens with an exhilarating mix of grit, humor, cell phones, and a well-turned lyric. Read this book—you'll be *very* glad you did."
—Kathleen Chalfant, actress

"These brave, amazing women are an inspiration to activists everywhere."   —Barbara Barrie, actress

Joan Wile - Peace!
Dec. 1, 2008

GRANDMOTHERS AGAINST THE WAR

Getting off Our Fannies & Standing Up for Peace

JOAN WILE

CITADEL PRESS
Kensington Publishing Corp.
www.kensingtonbooks.com

CITADEL PRESS BOOKS are published by

Kensington Publishing Corp.
850 Third Avenue
New York, NY 10022

All Kensington titles, imprints, and distributed lines are available at special
quantity discounts for bulk purchases for sales promotions, premiums, fund-
raising, educational, or institutional use. Special book excerpts or customized
printings can also be created to fit specific needs. For details, write or phone
the office of the Kensington special sales manager: Kensington Publishing Corp.,
850 Third Avenue, New York, NY 10022, attn: Special Sales Department;
phone 1-800-221-2647.

First printing: May 2008

10 9 8 7 6 5 4 3 2 1

Printed in the United States of America

Libraery of Congress Control Number: 2008921056

ISBN 13: 978-0-8065-2873-1
ISBN 10: 0-8065-2873-7

To my extraordinary grandchildren, Livia, Craig, Emily, Jake, and Michael, who were my main motivation for what little I've done to try and end the war. May they live in peace. ～

Contents

The Mothers

by Frances Whitmarsh Wile (my grandmother)
published during the First World War

My boy has donned the khaki
And taken gun in hand:
He heard the bugles calling,
The nation's high command.
His manhood and his future
He gives his native land.

I would not bar the threshold
Nor hold him from his place,
Though all the life I live by
Is in his eager face.
My sacrifice is offered
For freedom of the race.

No star that lights our banner
But rose upon the sky
Because, in countless thousands,
The boys went forth to die,
We answer to the bugles,
My fair-faced boy and I.

But O, some German mother,
Across the death-strewn sea,
Hath sent her son to battle—
As dear as mine to me.
To fatherland and kindred
She gives unflinchingly.

Her heart or mine, it may be,
Must break when they shall meet:
Upon the hearts of mothers
The marching footsteps beat:
On riven hearts of mothers
Must fall the charging feet.

Foreword
by Malachy McCourt

Joan Wile is the founder of Grandmothers Against the War and is a member of the Granny Peace Brigade—and at the proud age of 76, she has written a book. Let me be quite clear about one thing: Joan has written nice things about me here, but that is no reason for me to write nice things about her—I'm doing it because this is one hell of a book

Imagine a group of elderly women terrifying the Marine, Army, and Navy recruiters at the Times Square recruiting station. These huge strapping lads had to lock the doors and cower under their desks while the grannies demanded to be let join the armed forces. The poor lads had to call the police to rescue them! So come on, read this book and embark on a wild ride that made me cheer, made me weep in frustration, and made me laugh, watching Joan and her indefatigable gang of moral saboteurs lead us in the march against the despots, never allowing despair to darken their souls.

Chronicled here is the unending saga of brave women usually viewed by society as washed up, yet here they are: demonstrating, vigiling, singing, and getting arrested. Through their actions, they emulate our country's founders, who pledged their lives, their honor, and their fortunes in the cause of freedom. The founders are called our "forefathers" and 'tis rare for "foremothers" to be mentioned, so no better time than now.

This is a book of passion, compassion, music, and humor, encompassing our times of distress, yet filling us with hope and optimism for building the USA of our dreams. Give this book to your grandmother. Read it to your children and grandchildren. Follow the grandmothers to peace. ⌒⌒⌒

Introduction

WHEN I WAS A KID, anybody over thirty seemed to me to be off the radar screen—not worthy of my attention or even my acknowledgment. They were dim presences who supplied physical sustenance, scolds, and occasional gross kisses. They were totally irrelevant, as far as I was concerned. After all, their lives were essentially over, weren't they?

But now I'm seventy-six and, therefore, according to my twisted little child's logic, one of those irrelevancies myself. But, wait a minute. My life isn't over. It's still meaningful and exciting. I look forward to each day and what it will bring, or, more to the point, what I can bring to *it*.

In this book, I will endeavor to spark that kind of optimism and energy in others who think themselves to be over the hill, incapable of playing a vital role any longer. I'm able to present this outlook not only because of my own experience but mostly because of a number of other elders I've observed close up in the political action group, Grandmothers Against the War, which I founded and direct, and the Granny Peace Brigade, of which I am a proud member. We old broads mean to dispel the myth once and for all that, when we reach sixty or seventy or beyond, we don't matter any longer.

All of these women, some extending into the ninety-plus brackets, are so involved in activities dear to their hearts that I'm sure they would all say they've never been busier.

Despite hip and knee replacements, cancer surgery, loss of husbands and partners and even, in some cases, children, and other life crises, these women are full of life and plans for the future. Any older woman—I prefer the term "seasoned woman"—can be just as alive as they are. I hope our story offers you inspiration and insight as to how to make your later years productive and joyful.

At the same time, you will learn the remarkable story of a group of grandmothers, previously unknown to one another, who united together in a crusade to end the war in Iraq, tried to enlist in the military, got arrested, and went to *jail* for their cause. You will learn that one person *can* make a difference, at any age, and you'll learn how meaningful and vital your life can be! ❧

Acknowledgments

WHERE DO I BEGIN? So many people were responsible for making this book happen. Maybe I should begin with the then editor of michaelmoore.com, David Schankula, who began publishing my articles on that Web site, which were then read by Justin Hocking of Citadel Press, who approached me about writing a book. I owe Justin, as well.

I have so many grannies and supporters to thank, some whose names I don't even know, that it would take at least two pages to list them all. But, in addition to the seventeen grannies who joined me in getting arrested and jailed at the Times Square Recruiting Center in October 2005, whose names you will become very familiar with, there are many other people, in particular, that I'd like to mention: magnificent actors Malachy McCourt, Barbara Barrie, and Kathleen Chalfant; Congressman Charles Rangel; State Senator Bill Perkins, Manhattan Borough President Scott Stringer, City Council Member Gale Brewer, former New York State assemblyman and criminal court judge Frank Barbaro, Sally Connors, Mary Yelenick, Pat Constantino, Phyllis Cunningham, Nydia Leaf, Joan Pleune, Madelon Holder, Miriam Posner, Lorraine Krofchok; Judy Goldstein, Bernice Gottlieb; Greg Posnick, Lillian Pollak, Hugh Bruce, Pete Bronson, and the vigil Veterans for Peace; Fran Sears and Bob Sann, Professor Michael Flynn, Mark Manley, Marjorie Perces, and Frances Louis, who made many beautiful signs for our weekly vigil, colorful and eye catching. She did it even in the midst of serious eye surgery.

A special thanks, of course, to our dear friend, outstanding civil liberties attorney Norman Siegel, who defended us throughout our long trial and has continued to be a source of wise advice and support. Also, special thanks to his co-counsel during the trial, Earl Ward.

Another special thank you to the *New York Times* Metro Section columnist, Clyde Haberman, who was the first member of the press to notice us and wrote a terrific column featuring our vigil, the first of his three columns devoted to the Grannies.

To Judith Cartisano, my eternal gratitude. When I first got the idea to form Grandmothers Against the War, she, alone, encouraged me, and then accompanied me on the very first vigil. Without her, I doubt if I would have had the courage to proceed.

And, of course, my darling Citadel Press editor, Danielle Chiotti, who has been so sensitive to my story, and so thoughtful and wise in her suggestions for improving it.

I must also thank my excellent primary care physician, Dr. David Baskin, who kept my blood pressure normal during the stress of writing the book. It was a real challenge, believe me.

A final thank you to my partner, Herb Hecsh, who has helped in more ways than I can recount in tolerating my moods, my ups and downs, and, further, reassuring me when I had doubts and insecurities. ⌒〜

GRANDMOTHERS AGAINST THE WAR

— Chapter 1 —

Grandma Gets off
Her Tush

I was sitting around watching soaps
Just a useless old sad sack
Then I heard those Republican dopes
Say we had to bomb Iraq
 —from the song "Grannies, Let's Unite"*

"I've Got to *Do* Something"

IN THE MIDDLE OF THE NIGHT in September 2003, I awoke, very troubled. I had been increasingly upset about our invasion and occupation of Iraq since before Bush had launched the attack. Prior to its beginning in March 2003, I marched, I rallied, I signed petitions, I wrote letters to elected officials and newspaper editors, and was sickened when all my efforts and those of millions of people all over the world failed to stop Bush's mindless action. I became more and more distressed with each passing day as I began to see pictures of Iraqi children horribly wounded by our bombs and as I noted the rising death toll of our American kids fighting there. I was particularly horrified by a picture in *Time* magazine of a

*All lyrics and music for songs quoted in book by Joan Wile, ASCAP.

1

twelve-year-old Iraqi boy, Ali, who had lost both arms and was horribly burned over much of his body as a result of our bombings. In addition, this child had lost his entire family—mother, father, and many siblings. I thought to myself, "I've got to *do* something. I've got to try and stop this terrible war."

Redefining "Grandmother"

Well, I jumped up right out of my seat
Got my banners and peace signs out
Then I hurried down to the street
And started to yell and shout
—from "Grannies, Let's Unite"

Suddenly, the word *grandmother* popped into my head. "Wow," I thought, "that's a magic word. It connotes wisdom, love, nurturing, maturity, good common sense. People will take us seriously. They won't dismiss us as a bunch of drug-infused young radical kooks like they often did in the beginnings of the Vietnam resistance movement when the kids spearheaded the opposition. They'll pay attention." The words *Grandmothers Against the War* zoomed into my mind.

I had been an activist for brief periods throughout my life. It came somewhat naturally to me, inasmuch as I had been reared in the home of my uncle, Louis Bean, economic advisor to President Franklin Roosevelt's secretary of agriculture, and later vice president, Henry A. Wallace. Thus, I was infused at a tender age with Roosevelt's New Deal ideology. Another molding force was my maternal grandmother, Frances Whitmarsh Wile, who had been a suffragette in Rochester, New York, and had published her antiwar poetry, music, and a lyric still visible in the Episcopal Hymnal ("How Beautiful the March of Days"). She lived far away and died when I was eight so I hardly knew her but, years later, when I learned of her activist history and read her poems about the futility of war, the connections between us were so striking that I have come to believe there is such a thing as genetic inheritance of talents, and, yes, attitudes. After all, I have been a lyricist most of my adulthood, as well as an activist.

However, the pressures of my career as a singer-songwriter-musician and my duties as the single mother of two children kept me from any long-term political commitments. I'm ashamed to say that actually I was relatively unconcerned about the Vietnam War. My kids were babies then, and I was in the beginning stages of making headway in the music business. I didn't fully digest how wrongheaded the war was and, regretfully, the extensive death toll of our soldiers didn't get under my skin as it should have. I was *then* what I find so reprehensible about people *now*—apathetic.

In 2003, though, I was fully cognizant of the danger we posed to ourselves and the rest of the world by invading Iraq and was absolutely deadly serious about taking action. Thank God for e-mail! I was able to reach out to many people with like-minded sympathies about the Iraq catastrophe and organize a rally near my apartment at the beautiful Eleanor Roosevelt statue in Riverside Park, Manhattan. I set it for Saturday, November 22, 2003, and prayed for good weather—not too cold, and no rain.

God cooperated—she provided us with a lovely late fall day. Approximately fifty people showed up, including an assemblage of speakers I was able to corral famed Emmy Award–winner and Oscar-nominated actress Barbara Barrie (in the film *Breaking Away*, she played the mother, and she appeared as Brooke Shields's grandmother in the TV series *Suddenly Susan*), and a few local elected officials. I also invited my friend Marjorie Kadi to speak about Iraq, where she, an American, had lived for many years as the wife of an Iraqi diplomat. Marjorie knew a great deal about the history and culture of Iraq and was able to put our invasion into perspective, as

> *Strive not to "seem" but to "be."*
> —Vinie Burrows

its being one of many wrongheaded occupations perpetrated
on Iraq over the centuries. She enlightened us as to Iraq's
high level of art and knowledge and its unique archeological
sites. Too many Americans are unaware that Iraq is a highly
developed civilization—not, as some believe, a third-world
desert outpost. I was very impressed, also, with a speech given
by our then local New York State assemblyman Scott Stringer,
who later became the Manhattan borough president. He was
fiery and eloquent, in the spirit of his mother's cousin, the
great congresswoman Bella Abzug. I've always been grateful
to Scott for speaking at the rally. After all, I was someone
he'd never known or heard of. Another rousing speaker was
my dear old friend Judge Frank Barbaro, about whom I have
much to report on later.

I was also extremely pleased to have my oldest and youngest
grandchildren, Jake and Livia, at the rally, holding antiwar
signs. Hopefully, someday they will look at pictures of themselves from that day and be proud to have been such young
activists early in the movement to end the occupation of Iraq.

I felt the rally was a good beginning, but it was a one-
time event. I couldn't stop there; I had to do something on
an ongoing basis. Not long after the rally, I was hit with another middle-of-the-night inspiration—I would hold a regular vigil. I called a meeting in December of a few antiwar
women friends and posed the vigil idea to them. I wanted to
get started very soon, so as not to lose momentum from the
rally. Almost everybody pooh-poohed the idea. "It will be too

cold, winter's almost here," said one. "Nobody will show," cautioned another, and one person made the particularly helpful remark, "You're crazy!"

I was very depressed after they left, feeling I had started something that was just going to fizzle out having accomplished nothing. I called one of the meeting's attendees, my friend Judith Cartisano, the only one who had not expressed an opinion, and told her how disappointed I felt that nobody supported the idea. I thought maybe Judith, who had been active in the feminist movement during the '70s and '80s, might be up for another battle. "Despite the naysayers, I still believe it could work," I said, and to my immense relief, she replied, "I think so, too. Let's try it."

But, where to do it? Outside Grand Central Station? Penn Station? Lincoln Center? Each location seemed to present unsolvable problems—at the train stations, people would likely be in too much of a hurry either going to work or going home to notice, or during in-between times mostly not there; Lincoln Center would be only well attended at night, and so on. But Rockefeller Center had a spacious sidewalk and was flooded with tourists from all over the United States and the world. A quick check with the local police confirmed that it was legal to stand on the street side of the sidewalk (near the curb) and hold a vigil. I chose Wednesday afternoon from 4:00 to 6:00 P.M. That way, I'd catch the matinee crowd, tourists, and people going home from work all in one fell swoop. I set the date of the first vigil for January 14, 2004.

Two Little Grannies Standing in the Cold

The afternoon of our first vigil was possibly the coldest day in New York in years. Judith Cartisano and I went to Fifth Avenue in front of Rockefeller Center, each wearing two sets of gloves, layers and layers of clothing, and a homemade sign around our necks with the words *Grandmothers Against the War*. We were very nervous and apprehensive, expecting people to heckle us and, perhaps, push us around. One can feel very vulnerable making a controversial political statement in the middle of pulsating Manhattan crowds. Remember, in early 2004, an antiwar stance was not a majority opinion.

Although I originally planned for a two-hour vigil, we vigiled for only one—Judith or I dipping into a nearby building occasionally when the cold became too unbearable. It wasn't exactly a rip-roaring success, our little vigil, but we weren't jeered and insulted either. When Judith went inside to warm her hands and I was left alone on the street, I felt even more vulnerable. I had an instinct to take the sign off and pretend to be just another passerby. But, I charged up my guts as best I could and held my ground, praying for her to return as quickly as possible.

And then there were *three* little old ladies standing in the cold. The following week, another friend, Marjorie Perces, a dancer-choreographer in her eighties, joined us. Again, nobody aimed verbal darts at us; in fact, a few people smiled and gave us a thumbs-up gesture of support. We began to feel a little less uncomfortable in our new roles as public agitators. I soon reduced the time from two hours to one—it proved to be much too difficult to stand for more than an hour. Aged bones and joints react rather poorly to standing still for lengthy periods.

One day in February, a tall, nice-looking man strolled over and introduced himself as Clyde Haberman, a columnist for the *New York Times*. There were still only the three of us, but he interviewed us anyway. Shortly thereafter, the most wonderful article, "Heck, No? Antiwar Voices Persist, Softly," appeared in the *Times*, to a large extent featuring our little grandmothers' protest. Mr. Haberman humorously described our vigil. Among his comments, he noted that a passerby made a gesture as if he were shooting a gun at us, then quoted Judith who was not in the least bothered by the man's pretended assault, and said, "His aim was bad."

We Multiply

As spring and summer approached, our little vigil began to expand. I bought a white sheet at the Salvation Army for one dollar, washed it, then sewed it in half horizontally. Two of my grandchildren, Emily and Jake, and their friend Sebastian, helped print *Grandmothers Against the War*, in big, bold, multicolored letters.

Soon, our numbers totaled about six or seven on any vigil day. In July, a man approached us and introduced himself as Dennis Duggan, a columnist for *New York Newsday*. He told us he had been riding a bus down Fifth Avenue when he spotted our group holding the banner. Intrigued, he hopped off the bus and came over to interview us. Soon, another article about the grandmothers appeared, in *New York Newsday*, under his byline.

Shortly after that, a young Japanese woman, Miho Sakai, asked if she might film us for a segment to be broadcast on Japanese public television. It was quite a project—she filmed some of us in our homes and interviewed people at the vigil. Her television piece ran several times in Japan, we learned.

On the Avenue

A group of Veterans for Peace, headed by Peter Bronson, president of the New York City chapter, heard about our vigil and they joined us "on the avenue." They're still there today.

I can't tell you how much we like their being there every Wednesday. They make us feel secure and also give us an authenticity—it's not just old ladies standing there demanding an end to the war, it's veterans of wars, themselves, who, unlike most of the war makers in Washington, have actually experienced firsthand the horrors of combat. They can't help but command respect and serious attention.

Pete, a regular of our vigil, is a veteran of the Korean War, bearded, very serious and very dedicated to antiwar causes. He also has led the fight to keep the government from closing the Veterans Hospital in Manhattan. Another regular is Bill Steyert, a Vietnam vet. There isn't a vigil, an action, an arrest connected with the Iraq question that Bill hasn't been part of, he is so incredibly committed to ending the war and protecting our military people. Bill was one of the hundreds of people arrested for protesting during the 2004 Republican convention in New York City, who were imprisoned for as many as forty-eight hours in an old, dirty pier. They had to sit and sleep on an oil- and grease-ridden floor and were barely fed. Many of the lawsuits against the city are still pending in some cases, although a number have been settled with monetary compensation to the mistreated protesters!

The vets also lend some masculine saltiness to our vigil. Sometimes, one of them will call out within the earshot of passersby "What ever happened to Mission Accomplished?" Or, "How do you know when George Bush is lying?" And another vet will yell out, "His lips are moving!"

Soon, we began to sense growing support for our opposition to the debacle in Iraq. Some people applauded, some even joined us. We were particularly struck by the numbers of foreigners who gave us their approval. A woman from Spain told us, with a big smile, "I'm so glad to find you here. Until I saw you, I assumed all Americans supported Bush's war policy." A man from Italy came over to us one afternoon and gave each of us—by then twenty grannies—a kiss on the cheek. More and more often people stopped and photographed and filmed us. We were now a tourist attraction!

Once in a while, we were heckled. The most common remarks launched at us were, "Traitors" or "*I* support the troops." I found that very hurtful. How could we support the troops more than by trying to bring them home safely? This is indicative of the awful split this war has created among Americans. Sometimes, one of us would not be able to restrain his or her temper and would engage in a dialogue, sometimes heated, with an adversary.

Occasionally, a New York nut case, in which our city specializes, would give us a really hard time, often babbling incoherently. One such person began to hurl insults one day at one of our vets, Hugh Bruce, vice president of the New York City chapter of Veterans for Peace and a veteran of the Vietnam War. The man wouldn't stop, no matter what Hugh and the other vets said. Finally, Hugh had enough, grabbed the guy by the back of his collar, and marched him down to the end of the avenue where a policeman was standing. The heckler was taken to Bellevue Hospital, the usual repository for people having psychotic episodes.

Another time, Bill Steyert got into a verbal scuffle with a nasty heckler, and became so angry that I was afraid it would evolve into a physical confrontation, but it stopped short of that. Those are the only two occasions I can recall in the four-plus years of the vigil, which teetered on the brink of physical violence. Those few episodes aside, I would say we were a phenomenal success at peacefully alerting passersby to the crisis in Iraq. People from all over the United States and the world began snapping our pictures, some even videotaped and filmed us, giving us hope that our protest reached everywhere and thereby helping to dispel the notion that Americans were solidly behind the war. Perhaps, in our small way, we were able to counteract a bit the growing global antagonism (and, I'm afraid, well deserved) toward our nation. Maybe, just maybe, our little vigil had a long reach.

— *Chapter 2* —

Grannies Take Drastic Action

We were taken to the hoosegow
The judge said, "Pay your bail"
We said, "We ain't payin' nohow,
We'd rather stay in jail

You see, Judge, we've got to stay
'til they stop that gol-darn war,
someone's got to say
We won't take it any more"

—from the song, "The Granny Jailhouse Rock Blues"

Granny, Have You Gone off Your Rocker?

AFTER A YEAR AND A HALF, I began to face the unhappy fact that despite many protests, including ours, throughout the United States, Americans who opposed the war were not having an effect. Bush and his cronies were just as determined as ever to continue the war indefinitely. I felt that we had to do something more dramatic than the weekly vigil and the occasional mass marches we joined to get our urgent message across.

I heard that a group called the Raging Grannies of Tucson, Arizona, was arrested briefly in July 2005, when they attempted to enlist in the military at a local recruiting office. Even though they were released shortly thereafter and spent no time in jail, the story traveled all over the world. They were even on *The Today Show*. It occurred to me that if we were to do a similar action in New York City, the media capital of the world, it would possibly create an even greater press and media sensation and thereby help keep the issue alive. In the United States, unfortunately, to make your message heard, you have to think of strategies that will intrigue the television and newspaper people enough to come and cover you. I've learned that it's not enough to be passionately committed to a good cause and to create imaginative events; you have to become an expert publicist as well.

To get a group of grandmothers together who were willing to possibly be arrested and go to jail, I knew I'd have to contact other groups of activist grandmothers—there weren't enough in my vigil who would undertake such a risk. The first thing I did was to contact a Raging Granny who had occasionally come to my vigil, Corinne Willinger, figuring that if Raging Grannies in Tucson were willing to be arrested, probably Raging Grannies anywhere would be. Besides, her name had the word *willing* embedded in it!

I was right—Corinne leapt at the idea. A fierce opponent of the Iraq occupation, the seventy-eight-year-old was a long-time activist. Retired from her profession of teaching special

---

"Get your politics right, to get your thoughts straight, to figure out what this world is like and what you can do to make it better."
—Roz Boyd

education in the Bronx Psychiatric Center, Corinne, now widowed with four granddaughters, was devoted to her work with the Raging Grannies, a colorful organization founded in Canada in the '80s.

The Raging Grannies have a great sense of humor—they dress up in outlandish clothes and hats designed to caricature the ingrained concept of grannies as being sweet, slightly dotty, kitchen-bound, rocking-chair-attached old women. But their greatest distinguishing mark is their songs. Members of the group rewrite lyrics to very familiar songs, to express their political views. For instance, they've converted "Take Me Out to the Ball Game" to "Take Me Out of the War Game" with appropriate new lyrics. Corinne, herself, is a frequent lyricist for the Raging Grannies.

Corinne and I started reaching out, and again e-mail was a godsend. It enabled us to contact quickly and in great numbers potential granny jailbirds—we approached the Women's International League for Peace and Freedom, Grandmothers for Peace International, the Gray Panthers, Peace Action, the remarkably effective Code Pink, among others, in addition to my Grandmothers Against the War and Corinne's Raging Grannies. Before you could say "Bring the troops home now," eighteen seasoned women had assembled to enlist in the United States military.

We started having strategy meetings, and Norman Siegel, perhaps the best-known civil liberties attorney in America, volunteered to help us. I met Norman when a singing group I had formed, named the New York Granny Chicks, sang at one of his campaign parties to promote his run for New York City public advocate. Norman's involvement proved to be invaluable, as you will learn.

After much discussion, it was decided that we would attempt to enlist at the Times Square Recruiting Center, right in the heart of the theater district and virtually at the crossroads of

America, 42nd Street and Broadway. We picked Monday, October 17, and prayed for good weather. God cooperated once again by producing a beautiful sunny day.

Taking a Stand by Sitting Down

Promptly at 12 noon, eighteen grannies ranging in age from 59 to 90 approached the recruiting station doors, carrying buckets of cookies to dispense to the young soldiers working inside. We were greeted by about seventy-five supporters holding signs and banners and singing antiwar songs. But when we got to the door, it was locked. I rang the buzzer. Nobody answered. I rang again, but still nobody appeared. In fact, it looked as if nobody was inside at all. Just then, I saw a young man's head pop up from behind a desk and then quickly duck down again. Marie Runyon, our oldest granny at ninety, banged on the door with one of her canes, yelling, "Open up, come on, let's get cracking." Still no response. Wasn't it a shame they wouldn't allow us to enlist in the United States military? If we could so frighten our own tough soldiers that they cowered behind desks rather than face us, imagine what we could have done to the insurgents!

We had prepared a statement of purpose to read to the military personnel but, failing to get into the inner sanctum of the recruitment center, we turned around and faced the crowd of supporters and media filling the site and read it to them, each granny reading one sentence apiece.

We then decided to sit down on the ground as a form of peaceful, nonviolent protest. We laboriously settled ourselves on the concrete ramp in front of the recruiting center. This was quite difficult, given our ages and the various forms of arthritis and the other incapacitating muscular-skeletal infirmities of aging bodies. I took about five minutes to accomplish the task, for instance. But finally, fifteen of us were fully

STATEMENT OF THE ANTI-WAR GRANNIES
October 17, 2005

We are grandmothers heartbroken over the huge loss of life and limb in Iraq. We feel it is our patriotic duty to enlist in the United States military today in order to replace our grandchildren who have been deployed there far too long and are anxious to come home now while they are still alive and whole. By this action, we are not supporting the use of military force in Iraq—in fact, we are totally against it. But inasmuch as it exists, our goal in joining up is only to protect young people from further death and maiming.

We grandmothers have all had the privilege of living long lives and are willing to put ourselves in harm's way so that our own and other people's grandchildren will have a chance to enjoy full lives as we have.

We believe these young men and women are being used as cannon fodder in an illegal and totally unjusti-fied war against a nation which posed no threat to us. They were sent there on a web of lies and deceit result-ing in untold harm to them and countless innocent Iraqi people.

We hope that by enlisting today we can help bring about the early end of this immoral occupation and the return of our brave young people to their homes and families . . . now.

seated, the other three, supporting themselves with canes and walkers, standing right behind us. We sang our version of "God Bless America," renamed "God Help America," and chanted repeatedly, "We insist we enlist!"

It wasn't long before a bevy of uniformed policemen showed up and a beefy lieutenant announced through an impressive bullhorn that we were to disperse. Feeling we were doing nothing wrong, merely exercising our Constitutional rights to dissent, we remained where we were. Again, he asked us to disperse, and again we refused. Seeing we were at a definite impasse, and, I suppose, not knowing what else to do, the lieutenant asked his men to arrest us.

Getting up from the ground was an even more difficult proposition than getting down had been. In fact, for many of us it was impossible. I, for one, simply couldn't rise. But, I'm glad to report that New York's Finest, displaying tenderness and solicitude, helped lift up the more disabled grannies to their feet. One strong young policeman pulled me up by my armpits. They then handcuffed our hands behind our backs, asking in a caring manner, "Are these too tight?" or "Are they loose enough around your wrists?" With cameras flashing, we were escorted gently into two paddy wagons and removed to a nearby police precinct. As we were being led away, one of the grannies overheard a bystander remarking, "The cops here are the only ones with their original hips."

During this entire experience, I never for one moment considered the fact that I would be in jail for an indeterminate amount of time or perhaps eventually have to go to trial. The exhilaration of the moment overcame any such worries, and I, and all the other grannies, instead felt a glowing euphoria. We had stood—or rather, *sat*—our ground!

When we arrived at the police station, we were helped down from the paddy wagons and escorted inside, where we had our "mug shots" taken and then escorted up a flight of stone steps to an upper cell block. There, we were dispossessed of all our belongings, including our prescription glasses, our meds, and, even in one case, our shoelaces, and placed in jail, two per tiny cell. The heavy iron gates clanged shut. We were now prisoners. ⌒

— *Chapter 3* —

Seventeen Remarkable Women and Me

(From the Oldest to the Youngest)

> *I may be over the hill*
> *But I've got mountains left to climb*
> *Take away your clocks, I still*
> *Have lots of time, I'm in my prime*
> *Tomorrow when I'm young again*
> *Tomorrow when spring has sprung again*
> *Tomorrow when I begin again*
> *Tomorrow, tomorrow, tomorrow, when I win*
> *. . . again!*
>
> —from the song "Tomorrow, When I'm Young Again"
> (from the musical *Seven Ages of Woman*)

Meet the Grannies

WHO ARE THESE INCREDIBLE WOMEN, in their sixties through eighties, one even in her nineties, who would dare risk being arrested and going to jail for an unpredictable amount of time for a cause they so passionately believed in? It is really difficult to get the essence of each of my wonderful grannies in a few pages, as I will now attempt to do. One has to try and read between the lines to sense the pain and struggle they have undoubtedly often endured, and the courage they have exemplified. Here, then, are their stories told briefly in order from the oldest, Marie, to the youngest, Diane.

Marie

Marie Runyon is still beautiful at age 93, tall, slim, and patrician looking, with the bluest eyes; she is also the feistiest and most colorful of the grannies, her wit and clarity undiminished by her many years. Whenever a group of grannies is interviewed by the press or media, Marie is always out front, a star—not only because she is the oldest of us, but because her comments are so pithy, unvarnished, and even, at times, outrageous. Oh, did I mention that Marie is legally blind *and* very hard of hearing? Mere bagatelles, as far as she is concerned.

She is as unlikely a candidate as any for one of the saviors of Harlem, having been born in the hills of North Carolina. But, a savior she was of that beleaguered community. After serving a term as New York State assemblywoman for that legendary part of Manhattan, Marie founded the Harlem Restoration Project, which renovated and maintained Harlem buildings at affordable rents for residents of the area.

Prior to her political and housing advocacy careers, she had the most varied collection of jobs imaginable. Institutional psychologist, fund-raiser for progressive political causes, and copy reader for the *New York Post* (I'm sure she wouldn't be caught dead there now, given its sharp right turn into conservative politics) were just some of the things Marie did in her checkered past, as she likes to call it.

During her stint at the *Post*, she married her boss, the "slot man" at the copy desk, Damon Runyon's nephew Dick, with whom she had a daughter, dancer-choreographer Louise

("Weezie"). But, the marriage broke up when Weezie was two years old, and soon thereafter Marie moved into her current apartment in Morningside Heights. Oh, boy, thereby hangs a tale!

Thus began a more than forty-year fight with Columbia University to save her home in response to the university's efforts to demolish the building to make way for the Columbia College of Pharmacy. Year after year, Marie and a handful of tenants held their ground despite the lack of maintenance and crumbling apart of the building around them, as well as constant efforts by Columbia to evict the put-upon tenants. She even organized a "Rock-In," where people blocked the traffic in front of her building sitting in rocking chairs. In 2003, Columbia finally gave up and not only renovated the building entirely but broke through to Marie's neighboring apartment to give her extra space for an office, at no extra rent. The final symbol of Columbia's surrender was the plaque they placed on the exterior of the refurbished structure, which reads "Marie Runyon Court." Marie experiences the sweet taste of victory every time she enters her now elegant dwelling!

Marie was honored in 2007, when she received a Martin Luther King New York State Senior Award.

No bio about the Granny Peace Brigade would be complete without mention of grandchildren. Marie's are Brian, 29, a landscape designer, and Lucas, 24, an organic farmer and photographer.

Molly

Molly Klopot (*klopot* is Polish for "trouble," she says mischievously) is the quintessential grandmother. She is short, roly-poly, creased, and twinkling, and looks as if she would scoop you up in her arms on a moment's notice if she thought you needed solace. Her grandmotherly look and manner, how-ever, are merely window dressing. She is, in fact, a steely bundle of energy and determination awesome for an 89-year-old. She outwalks us, outstands us, outworks us to a shame-ful degree. The fact that Molly is legally blind doesn't faze her a bit.

This miniature powerhouse is a living embodiment of labor history in our country. Raised in Detroit, she saw the strug-gles to unionize the automobile industry. She remembers that, when she was 13, four 16-year-old friends were shot and killed during the Ford Hunger March. She witnessed the be-ginnings of the CIO and saw the United Auto Workers evolve into a powerful union. In fact, she and her young friends led the first UAW strike, teaching the workers songs and strate-gies, and supporting their lockdown inside the plant.

Molly speaks warmly of her upbringing in a very progres-sive Jewish family that was part of a tight-knit community where the children learned Yiddish and Jewish history and performed modern dance, sang in choirs, acted in plays, and produced art. "It was the most wonderful environment for a child," she says, eyes sparkling.

Molly wanted to be a doctor but was discouraged by her family physician who said there were three strikes against her: "You're Jewish, you're a woman, and you're poor," was his declared opinion. (How different from today's mores . . . we really *have* come a long way, Virginia.) Convinced that it would be practically impossible, Molly opted for majors in special education and psychology. After graduation, she passed a civil service exam and got a job in the beginning stages of the Social Security administration. She recalls how people laughed at the concept of getting paid by the government upon retirement but lived to see it become a treasured ben-efit of the American people.

As a young woman, Molly helped to organize a union of

the state, county and municipal workers of America. When World War II began, she went to work in a Ford factory, where she was the first woman to be elected a shop steward. There, she set up a women's committee, and one of her major accomplishments was to get the women to wear protective head covers so their hair wouldn't get dangerously caught in the machinery. When the matter was first brought up, they rejected the idea, for vanity reasons. Molly conceived the idea of a fashion show to see who could design the best hat or hair protection, and the women were won over. She also established a committee to obtain day care for the women's kids at the plant. We owe so much to these early pioneers like Molly in advocating women's issues, don't we?

After living in Texas and San Francisco, Molly got a scholarship to Columbia University, where she earned a master's in social work. She worked in that capacity in hospitals until her retirement, and was also an adjunct professor at New York University. In a forum she led on women's questions, she was attracted to one of her students, a union organizer, Morris (Moish) Klopot, who became her husband when they were both forty years old. The couple adopted their two children, a boy and a girl.

Molly's husband died in 1997. In that year, also, Molly started volunteering with the Women's International League for Peace and Freedom (WILPF), which she never fails to proudly point out in every interview is "the oldest and largest international women's peace organization in the world." When the chair of the New York chapter died, it fell to Molly to carry on in that position, which she does to this day. She still puts in full days at WILPF's Lower East Side offices, schlepping in all the way from Coney Island and back on the subway, very often late at night. We worry about Molly some, particularly given her poor eyesight, but she dismisses us with a wave of the hand when we voice our concerns, indicating the equivalent of a verbal, "Oh, pooh."

Molly has four grandsons, aged 13 to 26, which certainly accounts to an extent for her passionate opposition to the war in Iraq.

Lillian

Another elder made of steel, Lillian Rydell, at 88, is an incredible dynamo who puts us "youngsters" to shame with her boundless vigor. She is the president of the Westside chapter in New York of the National Peace Action Organization and is on the New York State board. In this capacity, she runs meetings and forums, puts together a newsletter, manages its fund-raising thrift shop, and does innumerable other tasks a person half her age would have difficulty carrying out. As if she doesn't have enough on her plate, she also works with the Granny Peace Brigade and Grandmothers Against the War. Lillian is our resident devil's advocate. She firmly questions our decisions and forces us to rethink our positions. Yes, Lillian is formidable sometimes, but she is often right, too.

Activism is nothing new to Lillian, who began her activist career when she became the first female dispatcher in the National Maritime Union, for which she got tons of publicity at the time. She had grown up in a small coal-mining town in Pennsylvania and moved to Baltimore during World War II to work at the Aberdeen Proving Grounds. When she went to work in the Maritime Union, she found her home, so to speak. As she says, "I was thrilled to be working for a union because I was raised to believe in the rights of working people." It didn't hurt that she met her first husband there, also, who was a merchant seaman.

Some years later, after moving to New York, Lillian worked

for about twenty years in the printing industry—from production to estimating to selling. During this time, she remained politically active and organized campaigns of all sorts. She was particularly active in the anti–Vietnam War movement and, before that, had opposed the Korean War. Lillian has always been and still is a leftist. We must treasure the Lillians of the world because they are the ones who fought for better benefits for the working class and to preserve basic rights for us all.

Lillian says, "I have a wonderful daughter and I've had two wonderful marriages. If I were to have it to do all over again, I wouldn't change a thing." How many of us can say that on the far side of our lives? They don't make people like Lillian Rydell anymore.

Vinie

Vinie Burrows is our celebrity, and we feel so privileged to have her among us. But, Vinie demurs at such a description. "Call me a star that shines continuously. Celebrities are like meteors that dazzle for an instant, then die out." She has been described by famous theater critic, Clive Barnes, as "one of the reigning divas of the Black Theater." We feel she is a reigning diva of *all* theater. Period. She is also our most eloquent spokesperson, with her stirring voice and articulate expression. When we are interviewed in a public setting, I urge Vinie to speak first on our behalf.

Petite and lovely, Vinie was born in Harlem Hospital, but she guards her age carefully. "I'm as old as my tongue and a little older than my teeth," she says. Vinie was a true Wunderkind. Her accomplishments as a child boggle the mind (as do her adult achievements, too, by the way). She graduated from Wadleigh High School in Harlem at the age of 15, a member of Arista (the national honor society for high school students), the possessor of a Classics Award for three years of Latin with a score of 99 out of 100, an American History Award for a score of 100 on the Regents, plus a prize for excellence in English composition and literature. Are you feeling as inadequate as I did when learning of these incredible academic triumphs?

Her mother was a member of the International Ladies Garment Workers Union and enrolled Vinie in drama classes for children of workers. As a result of this experience, Vinie worked in radio at New York City's WOR and WNYC stations. While still in her teens, she auditioned with a hundred girls for a role in the Broadway production of *Wisteria Trees*, starring Helen Hayes. Vinie was chosen, thereby beginning a career as actress, playwright, director, and producer that spanned the next sixty years. In rapid succession came six more Broadway shows— *Green Pastures* with Ossie Davis; *Skin of Our Teeth*, with Helen Hayes, Mary Martin, and George Abbott; *Jezebel's Husband*, with Claude Rains and Ben Gazzara; *Mrs. Patterson*, with Eartha Kitt, Alberta Hunter, and Avon Long; *The Ponder Heart*, by Eudora Welty, with David Wayne and Will Geer, and *Mandingo*, with Franchot Tone and featuring Dennis Hopper in his first Broadway role.

While in Berlin on a State Department tour with luminaries Ethel Waters, Lillian Gish, Martha Graham, Eileen Heckart, and Thornton Wilder, among others, Vinie conceived the idea of writing and acting in one-woman shows, eight of which she famously went on to perform on the New York stage and in more than six thousand performances in colleges and theaters on four continents.

Vinie has been honored with numerous important awards both in the theater and for her work for the United Nations as a permanent representative for the Women's International Democratic Federation. Not one to rest on her many laurels, however, Vinie, at the age of 75, returned to study at her alma mater, New York University, graduating summa cum laude with a master's in performance studies. In May 2007, she received an honorary doctorate from Paine College, a historic black college in Augusta, Georgia, at their commencement convocation.

Doctor Vinie has two children, five grandchildren, and three great-grandkids. She is still very much a full-time working actress, having closed recently in an off-Broadway production of the Greek tragedy *Hecuba*, and a regional production of a new play, and scheduled as of this writing to act in a "site-specific" play in Manhattan. Impressive, wouldn't you say?

Corinne

Corinne Willinger is one of our brigade members who is also a Raging Granny; not only that, but she writes a number of ingenious lyrics to some of the songs they sing. A very clever and quietly accomplished woman, Corinne grew up in the Bronx, New York City, in an apartment house on a tree-lined street and near a small park (New York City isn't all sun-blocking canyons of steel skyscrapers). Her father, whom she worshipped from afar, was a quiet, stoic man who was always reading. He was the oldest of eight brothers, all bald when still young, who came to the United States when he was six months old. They had little money, but her dad was able to attend Columbia University School of Dentistry, though he never graduated from high school. In those days, one could take a test and if you passed and were accepted, you could attend dental school. Before becoming a dentist, he had been a trolley car conductor and cab driver.

Corinne's mother was one of seven children in a closely knit family. Her father had been a carriage maker in Russia and became an auto worker in this country, for which the family was very proud because he was one of very few Jews then allowed to hold that kind of job.

The great family tragedy occurred when Corinne was 16. In 1945, just before the end of World War II, her only sibling, a brother, who had enlisted in the army after two years of college, was reported missing. He had been stationed in Metz, France, behind the battle lines, and had gone on a 24-hour pass, never to be seen again. The family did everything they could think of to find him; however, the army gave up searching for him after one year, despite the fact that her father went to Washington to plead with them to continue the search. They had posters made offering American cigarettes (a very valuable postwar commodity) for any information about him and his whereabouts, and had a distant relative who was stationed in France get them posted in the area. All efforts proved futile. No body was ever found.

Her father soon after developed leukemia, which Corinne blamed partly on a faulty X-ray machine. The dangers of X-rays were relatively unknown at the time. Her dad began losing weight; from a tall robust man, he grew gaunt and was disappearing before her eyes. Corinne always connected the loss of her father with her brother's disappearance. He died in 1949.

Partly in an effort to escape the tragedy, she became active politically, joining an organization called American Youth for Democracy, which defended the Soviet Union during World War II and fought the encroachment of the anticommunist McCarthy era.

At nineteen, she married a young man whom she had known for a few years and was just discharged from the navy, and she then completed her bachelor's degree from Hunter College. In 1951, while pregnant with her first child, her husband and she received a visit from two young men from the FBI, who invited them to visit their office and talk to them and, when they refused, warned them to be careful. As soon as the two agents left, Corinne and her husband rushed to gather all papers they thought might implicate them in "deviant political activity" and flushed them down the toilet.

Soon after, Corinne's first child was born, a beautiful little girl. Twenty-two months later, Corinne gave birth to her second child, a long, thin, bright, active boy. They moved to New Rochelle, where she became a substitute teacher, then began working as a preschool teacher and later director of the Mount Vernon YMHA nursery school while attending and graduating from Bank Street College of Education. In 1970, she began working at Bronx Psychiatric Center in a preschool program called "Parent and Child Education." The patient/client was the mother (or at times, the father); and the center ran a nursery school for children from 2 to 5 years old, and a parent education program. (The director of the program was Dr. Carolyn Goodman, whose son Andrew was murdered, along with two other young men, James Chaney and Michael Schwerner, in Mississippi in 1963 in a nationally known case.) In 1981, Corinne went on to teach adult patients at the adult education program at Bronx Psychiatric Center and taught there until her retirement in 1990, after working at the hospital for twenty years.

From 1972 to 1975, she went through a very difficult divorce. Her husband, who after World War II had started with his brother a business manufacturing paraphernalia for tropical fish had accumulated money that he was unwilling to share with her. He had her followed; she had him followed. It almost became a story worthy of a Hollywood B-movie, except that to Corinne it was a devastating experience. They were divorced in 1975, and she married her second husband a year later. Together, they became very involved in labor politics and actively opposed the Vietnam and Gulf wars.

But by 1992, it became obvious that her second husband had early symptoms of Alzheimer's disease. He, himself, diagnosed his problem in 1991, although his doctor told him his problems were merely age related. His memory and behavior worsened and his physical disabilities progressed. She put him in a nursing home in 1996 and he died in 1997.

After his death, she began devoting more time to her children and grandchildren. Her daughter, a vocational rehabilitation counselor in a women's prison, lives in Connecticut with her husband and "lively, lovely" 14-year-old daughter. Corinne's son, a law school graduate, runs his father's and uncle's business and is a part-time jazz guitarist. He has two girls, ages 23 and 20; one attends Tulane University and the other recently became assistant editor at the Condé Nast magazine called *Lucky*. Another granddaughter is a 21-year-old student at the University of Southern California.

Corinne is dedicated "to actively work to improve the lives of those struggling to survive, raise families and live a good life in a healthy, peaceful world."

Betty

Betty "Coqui" Brassell is the poster girl of the Granny Peace Brigade. Partly it's because of her walker, of course. It's a dramatic representation of the fact that we are old grandmothers liable to have the usual disabilities of age. But it also has to do with the flowers she always wears in her hair and her beautiful hair itself, the epitome of "snowy white." She projects the perfect granny image for any cameraman who wants to have his pictures stand out, and she's featured in just about every newspaper photo we've ever had, as well as up front in all the television coverage, too.

Betty, a Southern woman at heart, has many remarkable qualities. Unlike the other members of the Granny Peace

Brigade, Betty had little formal education—she had to drop out of school early to go to work. However, this has no bearing on her importance to the brigade. Betty is admired by all of us for her strength, her dedication, her courage, and her intelligence.

Despite her inability to walk without a walker, Betty has gone everywhere with us—including Germany. She made the entire trek from New York to Washington in the summer of 2006, as well, and attends every single event we concoct. Sometimes, when on a very long march, or while crossing the Brooklyn Bridge on Grandparents Day, for instance, she uses a wheelchair, but most of the time, she walks.

Betty was born in the Deep South in January 1930 in the small town of Wrens, Georgia, but moved as a baby to Augusta. Her section of town had the bizarre name of Pinch Gut. Later, she lived in Frog Hollow, Georgia. It doesn't require too much imagination to picture in one's mind these colorful-sounding hamlets, does it? When Betty was a little girl, her mother left her father and moved with her and her sister, Frances, to Asheville, North Carolina, where she worked in a clothing establishment. "She was a very good dressmaker," according to Betty.

Her mother died when Betty was six years old, and she was returned to her father, who was, as Betty says, "a good man when he was at work or asleep." After a rough childhood, she escaped at 18 into an early marriage, which she describes as "a war zone," followed by the birth of her daughter when she was 19 and the birth of her son at 21. When her children were six and four, respectively, Betty fled yet again, this time to New York, to escape her bad marriage. She had exactly forty dollars to her name and stayed with her sister until she got on her feet. After a year, she got a job at AT&T as a telephone operator—first as a domestic one, then an international one—and ultimately, in radio and television for seventeen more years until her retirement. It was then that her life took an unexpected and extraordinary turn.

Betty inquired of a local Democratic leader about a problem she had in her public housing project. One thing led to another and, before she knew it, she was involved in local politics. Before the incident, she had never even voted, but soon she became well versed in civic matters and started participating in protests in the streets, organized by her local district leader, Rosie Mendes, and her city councilwoman, Margarita Lopez. Betty took pictures of the various events, starting her important lifelong task of recording the peace and justice activities in which she participates, and thus documenting pieces of history.

In 2000, Betty joined Ms. Lopez on a trip to Vieques, Puerto Rico, as one of a hundred volunteers investigating the dangerous U.S. nuclear testing that was being conducted there. On April 7, Betty traveled to Vieques, where she had the adventure of her life. She and her companions endured many hardships, sleeping on the ground, getting into dangerous situations. In one particularly dramatic escapade, Betty sneaked herself and her cameras through U.S. Navy security, in an effort to find the Salgado-Sanae family that had been held virtually under house arrest for eleven years.

In 1989, Hurricane Hugo had destroyed all the houses in this family's neighborhood except for theirs. Because that house was intact, the navy wanted it to house some of their own personnel. The navy bulldozed the other houses and forbade the residents to return, so they could grab the land for their own purposes. They tried again and again to make a deal with the Salgado-Sanae family to vacate, but Petra, the woman who headed the family, refused. Finally, the navy put a fence around the house and forbade them to leave or have people come to see them. Betty was shocked and outraged. She couldn't believe her own government could do the things that she learned they did in Vieques. She had found her mission. She took hundreds of pictures and made videotapes of Petra's "imprisonment," and when she returned to New York, she showed the pictures everyplace she could—colleges, universities, bookstores, even at street tabling events. She also spoke on WBAI and other radio stations about Vieques.

She then codeveloped a penpal program with a first grade teacher whereby the students in the Manhattan school exchanged letters with pupils in a Vieques school. Betty traveled back and forth between New York and Vieques, taking photos and videos of the kids in the program, and was able to get several newspaper stories and a four-day ABC-TV segment, hosted by Art McFarland, about the project.

Betty is very proud of the name bestowed on her by some of the people she helped in Vieques—"Coqui"—which is the name of the symbol of Puerto Rico, a tiny, tiny frog with a big beautiful voice that sings at night, especially in rain, and makes a sound like the word *coqui*. She prefers to be known by that name rather than her legal name, Brassell. We love the name, too, because it is a symbol of what she so perfectly represents—an ordinary person with a voice big enough to make her cause heard.

Betty's importance to the Granny Peace Brigade can't be underestimated. She is the unofficial shutterbug of all our events and activities, and has produced hundreds and hundreds of pictures detailing what we've done from our beginnings onward.

Betty is proud of her two children. Her daughter, a college graduate, has a management job in Florida and plays several instruments. She also makes flutes and flute bags. Her son has a son who has a son, thereby making Betty one of our three great-grandmothers.

Joan

Wow, this is an opportunity of a lifetime—writing my own bio. Can anybody among us resist this golden chance to fully indulge one's ego? I've got to be careful not to blather on about myself to an unseemly degree.

I was born in 1931 in Rochester, New York, to Janet, a 20-year-old philosophy major, and Lou Meltzer, a 23-year-old cellist with the Rochester Philharmonic Symphony. I've been told by people who knew his playing that he was a phenomenal musical talent. My parents split when I was a baby and I was sent to live with my mother's oldest sister in the Washington, D.C., area, who was married, as mentioned earlier, to a leading policymaker in the Roosevelt New Deal.

I went back to live with my mother at age seven, when she remarried. When I was eleven, my stepfather went off to war and then decided not to return to us. I loved him very much; that quite simply broke my heart and I don't think I ever got over it. He had been a loving father to me during the four years he had lived with us. In fact, he had adopted me legally. But, I hardly ever saw him again after that time.

I was also very negatively affected by an experience in junior high school in Arlington, Virginia, where we then lived. In an effort to cope with my grief over my stepfather's abandonment, I began a school newspaper. I couldn't seem to get any teacher to be a faculty adviser, and finally had to do everything myself—writing, raising funds, and printing, When it was ready, I proudly distributed the paper to all the student body one morning. But, at lunch in the cafeteria, I was pelted with wads of my newspaper and food. I heard the words "Dirty Jew" and "Kike." Until then, I never thought of myself as a Jew and still don't know how they got that idea. It's true, my father was a Jew, as was my maternal grandfather, but I was raised by my mother's sister and my mother, who had been, in turn, raised by their gentile mother. A mystery. It was the most mortifying experience of my young life. I wanted the ground to swallow me up. A very nice Catholic girl named Ethel took me to the bathroom where she tried to comfort me until my mother came to retrieve me. I stayed out of school for about two weeks, and I heard that the principal, Ira Beatty (Warren Beatty's and Shirley MacClaine's father, as it so happens) had made some sort of token admonition over the loudspeaker system and suggested that the cruel boys who had abused me call me to apologize. Only one did.

I learned a year later, after I had switched schools, what had really happened. I was acting with the Arlington Little Theatre, and went to a cast party attended by Mr. Beatty and his wife. I asked Mr. Beatty why I couldn't get any faculty help. He told me that he had orders from the Arlington school board to "keep that Jew off the paper." (How did *they* know I was three-quarters Jewish blood, come to think of it?) I've always suspected that he had instigated the attack on me in the cafeteria. I feel certain that such great progressives as Warren and Shirley would not have been pleased at their father's acquiescence to the school board's anti-Semitic request. That experience, plus my outrage at sitting on public buses where black people had to sit in the rear, soured me on living in the South, and I couldn't wait to get out.

By the way, the following year, after I'd left the school, the newspaper I'd founded won a Virginia State prize.

Right after my seventeenth birthday and after only three years of high school, I escaped to the University of Chicago. The U. of C. had a special program in those days by which every year they admitted about two hundred students without high school diplomas into the college if they could successfully pass their entrance exams. One of my classmates was Mike Nichols, another was Susan Sontag, and others included some of the people who formed the first Second City ensemble: Ed Asner, a war vet; Tony Holland; and Severn Darden. Fritz Weaver, the actor, was a graduate student in history after his return from his stint working in mental hospitals as a conscientious objector.

My biological father, Lou Meltzer, had four other children whom I saw every year or two when I visited him. He was quite an amazing man. He left the symphony while in his thirties and went to New York City, where he became a comedy writer for radio. He wrote for all the great shows—*Duffy's Tavern, Fred Allen, Oscar Levant,* and many others; and when television took over the airwaves, he moved successfully into that area, as well. He created the first late-night comedy show, though it is seldom credited as such, *Broadway Open House.* He worked for Sid Caesar, for Red Skelton, and more. To me, he was always a very glamorous but distant figure to whom I was never able to get close.

Just before finishing my BA in Chicago, I moved to Manhattan because of my burning ambition to be a jazz singer. After many struggles, typical of showbiz wannabes, I finally became a working singer, doing cabarets, TV and much studio work (jingles, records, movie soundtracks). I had many disappointments, worked many gin mills and lounges along the way, but also had many great gigs that were exciting and enjoyable. Many stand out, but a particularly memorable one occurred on the night before the McGovern/Nixon presidential election, when I sang to a huge assortment of luminaries my original song "Come Home America," on the stage of the Palace Theatre in a gala event coordinated by vice presidential candidate Sargent Shriver.

One of the low points? It would have to be the night I was sent for hours by bus to a pool hall way out in New Jersey and had to duck under a bar and climb onto the stage where the piano was perched somewhat precariously, to sing and play to the accompaniment of loudly clacking billiard balls.

I began writing lyrics and music and wrote some songs for films, records, and TV shows, as well as hundreds of jingles. In my later years, I wrote six musicals, four of which were produced Off- and Off-Off-Broadway. Professionally, I am proudest of that accomplishment, particularly my show *Seven Ages of Woman*, which has often been performed in a number of different productions, one with Tony Award–winner Shirley Knight, and some with my daughter and me. When she turned twelve, my granddaughter, Emily, a superb singer, was added to the family version.

I married twice, first to a drummer and songwriter, Herb Wasserman, with whom I had two children: Ron, now the principal bassist with the New York City Ballet Orchestra (string players run in my family!) and occasional player with the New York Philharmonic when the ballet is off season, and Diana (DeeDee), a speech therapist who works at several hospitals and nursing homes in New York and northern New Jersey. I'm very proud of my daughter, who despite losing a breast to cancer at the young age of thirty-one while her children were very small, persevered to get a master's degree in speech pathology and was able to create a valuable professional career beginning in her early forties. My second marriage, at age 47, was to one of my college boyfriends whom I hadn't seen for twenty-five years. An old story, I guess— reliving one's youth. Unfortunately, I didn't know that, attractive and smart as he was, he was a serious alcoholic. That marriage was a brief one. I had moved to California to live with him but, fortunately, had kept my apartment in New York. Otherwise, I would probably have had to move to Yonkers when I returned—not that there's anything intrinsically wrong with Yonkers, mind you. Moral: If you have to move from

Manhattan, do *not*, I repeat, do *not*, ever, ever, give up your apartment!

I have five grandchildren, ages 12, 14, 14, 18, and 21, all extremely gifted, but I'd better stop now on this subject before I make an obnoxious spectacle of myself.

Carol

Carol Husten is our Bombshell Granny. She has such a powerful personality, it's impossible to ignore her. When she speaks, in her husky, Brooklyn-tinged voice, we all stop talking and listen. Carol is a whirlpool of ideas, a cascade of imagination. It is no wonder that she presided as chair of Peace Action New York State (PANYS) for several years. It is also no wonder that Carol has been a very astute and successful businesswoman. That is just part of her range, as you will learn—the woman is full of surprises.

She was born in 1931 in Brooklyn but soon moved to Long Island, where she spent her formative and high school years. She describes glowingly her childhood: "I have to tell you I was definitely not an underprivileged kid. Besides loving parents, I had everything and more." Not many of us were so fortunate, I suppose, and Carol's strength and self-assurance reflect her happy upbringing. She went to Russell Sage College in Troy, New York, where she met her husband, Harvey Husten, a radio personality there. After graduation, they set up housekeeping in Haddonfield, New Jersey, where he was a radio jazz disc jockey and also program director. She taught health and physical education and had two children, Larry and Amy, who are only ten and a half months apart. In other words, she became pregnant again six weeks after her son was born! Whew!

Tragedy struck Carol for the first time in her life at the

> *"Along with the love and responsibilities, a woman must be a teacher. Teach children to be respectful, honorable and live with principles, to be a participant in the world and recognize people for who they are and not for who you are told they are."*
> **—Judy Goldstein**

age of 26, when her 32-year-old husband died of phlebitis after a bout of kidney stones. As a young widow, she was scooped up by her supportive parents, who took in Carol and her young children, thus helping her to cope with this awful trauma. Despite the misfortune of losing her husband so early, Carol's determination to care for her two toddlers helped her keep her head above water and move forward.

But, another terrible blow soon befell her when her beloved father died a year and a half later. Now in charge of supporting her mother and her children, Carol took over operation of her father's fine printing paper business. She ran the company for ten years, before selling it and going back to school to earn a degree in guidance. She returned to teaching, at James Madison High School in Brooklyn, where she taught in a special program for potential dropouts and truants. Big-hearted Carol loved the kids, and therefore must have been extremely effective in turning them around.

When her own kids went off to college, she moved to Brooklyn and bought a brownstone. Realizing what a great way it was to make money, she bought another . . . and another . . . and another . . . until she owned six and managed two additional ones. She invested with her sisters and friends. Carol had daring, discipline, and a very good head for business. She was a veritable Donald Trump!

Eventually she sold all of the buildings, except for the one she currently lives in and another she had purchased by herself. Becoming bored with her reduced business enterprises, Carol went back to teaching, this time kids who were mentally challenged. At 65, she retired again to pursue her career as a volunteer activist.

She had been a World Federalist in college but, like me during the VietnamWar, was too busy raising her babies, working, and trying to have a social life to get much involved with the antiwar movement. However, when her kids went to college, she became politically active, first with SANE and then with Peace Action, the successor to SANE. Since no one volunteered to take on leadership roles, Carol did, and eventually became chair, as previously mentioned. She stepped down a couple of years ago to encourage younger people to run the group. However, she still chairs fund-raising and is very involved with programming and development. Between all these chores and her work with the Granny Peace Brigade, Carol is one of the busiest people I know.

But perhaps the most surprising thing Carol has done came after she got involved with the Granny Peace Brigade. Once we began to do a little performing—my songs and a Granny chorus line—Bev Rice said one day, "I'd love to do a comedy routine as Barbara Bush!" But, she backed off and spunky Carol jumped in instead. I wrote the routine, and Carol helped with ideas and lines.

It takes very big guts to do stand-up comedy alone, at any age. But to do it for the first time at age 74 is beyond gutsiness. The minute Carol came onstage in her blue suit, white fright wig, and big pearls, she had the audience laughing, and she's gotten better and better with each performance.

Carol has two grandchildren—Harry, 4, and Max, 8. She says jubilantly: "My world spins around them. I am one of the luckiest women on the earth. I truly feel that way and that is why I feel I must stay involved so the world will be here for them and all future generations."

Carol Husten—real estate magnate, teacher, peace activist, *and* stand-up comic! How's that for diversity?

Barbara Walker

It's amazing how a chance meeting can totally change one's life. My encounter with Barbara Walker on the Manhattan 104 bus was like that.

It was shortly after I'd begun the Grandmothers Against the War vigil. She was already on the bus when I got on, and she spotted a button I wore at the time on my backpack, "Where's the Outrage?" It just happens that she'd been ruminating on that very theme when she noticed it. She came over to me and said that she appreciated the button and how it expressed so well her feelings. I told her about my weekly vigil and invited her to attend. Little did Barbara know that as a result of that casual conversation, she would ultimately land in jail, be on trial for six days, travel twice to Germany, go on a ten-day trek to Washington, give speeches, be featured in articles in her local paper, the *Staten Island Advance*, and, most surprising of all, costar in a play (more about that in my description of our Granny Cabaret Show)!

Barbara is a standout beauty. She is quite tall, of a golden light brown hue, with marvelous sculpted features. She has the kind of personality that is so charming and friendly and totally unconfrontational that it can honestly be said that she is immensely well liked by all.

Barbara has lovely memories of her early childhood in Harlem—sitting on the windowsill at the fire escape, waiting for her mother to return from her job as a court stenographer, for instance. Walks with her Nana. Going to her nearby Salem Church. Her father was a policeman, and a lasting memory was seeing him helping a runny-nosed, apparently temporarily incapacitated man who was slouched on a stoop.

In 1939, she and her brother, Teddy, moved from Harlem to Jamaica, Queens, where they were raised. Her idyllic childhood was tragically altered when her mother died six months after giving birth to a little girl, four days before Pearl Harbor Day, December 7, 1941. Barbara was 8.

She and her siblings were cared for by her cousin Ethel until her father remarried. Unfortunately, her father's new wife turned out to be the proverbial wicked stepmother of fairy tales. Her one positive contribution was Barbara's brother, Albert.

Barbara graduated from Hunter College ("For us, it was Smith College on the Independent subway line," says Barbara) and hitchhiked around Europe on an extended leave of absence while working with the Institute of International Education. Years later, she worked with the United Nations, principally in the areas of education exchange programs and peacekeeping missions. Her UN posts required her to live in Addis Ababa, Ethiopia, where she raised her son, David, now a State Department employee. She lived later in Namibia and was also posted in Jerusalem. Barbara retired in 1993, then worked on certain interesting programs at UN headquarters for a number of years. She is on the board of directors of the Richmond County Orchestra—in addition to her work with the Grannies. Barb has four grandchildren, each of whom is, as she says, "unequivocally adorable." Gosh, where have I heard that before?

Barbara Harris

If ever there was an example of a person overcoming a difficult environment to become a valuable, inspiring citizen and high professional, it is certainly our lovely Barbara Harris. She

is sylphlike, elegant, and beautiful, but her strength of character is a core part of the inner Barbara. Though she pre-
sents the demeanor and look of a lady with a very proper
and comfortable upbringing, in actuality she started life as a
troubled youth in a Bronx housing project. She is absolutely
the antithesis of her beginnings.

From the start of kindergarten, she was a latchkey child;
both parents worked and her older sister by eight years paid
little attention to her. She recalls walking home by herself
from kindergarten at lunch and eating while listening to *The
Romance of Helen Trent* and *My Gal Sunday* on radio, the pre-
cursors to television soaps. This resonates with me loudly, as
one of my childhood memories is that of listening to those
same programs when I would be home from school due to
illness. Ann Shirazi and I were also latchkey children, causing me to wonder if some of the activism we three have done
as adults can be traced at all to childhood neglect and lone-
liness.

Barbara began "acting out" in school in the sixth grade.
She had always been a good student prior to that, showing
a high aptitude in math and science especially, but she started
to dislike school and caused trouble as a result. She played
hooky, threw things out of classroom windows, refused to
walk in line, and generally was disruptive. She was often sent
to the principal's office for her behavior, where she was made to
copy pages from the dictionary for an hour or so. In spite of
this punishment, she says, "I am still a poor speller." She
caused a particular amount of trouble in her home economics class. She got her cooking group to call itself the "Burnt
Bagels" when the other groups preferred the "Happy Home-
makers" or the "Cupcakes." (I have to admit that Barbara,
with that sort of witty swipe at authority, was the kind of kid
I would have liked to hang out with, having been a trouble-

maker in school myself.) She failed her home economics term project, which was to prepare a book called "My Dream Home." She had only one page—a bedroom, and a dark bedroom at that.

But Barbara was finally pointed in the right direction by her high school homeroom teacher, Miss Harlo, who provided encouragement and instilled in Barbara a sense of her worth as an intelligent and capable girl. Without Miss Harlo's championship of her, she feels she would never have overcome her obstacles. Miss Harlo's nurturing of Barbara illustrates how vital it is for every child to have at least one authority figure to believe in him or her, particularly, as in Barbara's case, if that kind of support is not supplied by parents.

Although Barbara married at 19 and quickly had two daughters, she went to night school and managed to get a BA in Education (1963) and a master's degree in business and labor relations from the New School for Social Research in 1982.

She had a most impressive and varied career—she began teaching in the public school system and at the Pleasantville Cottage School for emotionally disturbed children, but joined AT&T in 1969, where she learned to design early computer programs. She moved up at AT&T, eventually becoming a corporate education trainer and then the manager of Support Services National Training Program, which involved course development, training teachers, and delivering advanced classes. She was trained as a corporate quality manager and team facilitator and participated in labor relations issues.

Barbara is particularly proud of the initiatives she helped create at AT&T for women—alternative part-time and flex-time schedules, as well as programs providing support and information for new parents. Her final job was teaching English as a second language (ESL) at the New School, where she received her teaching certificate in 1992. Well deserved, I'd say.

In the midst of her busy career, Barbara, beginning in the '60s, was very politically active, sparked by SANE antinuclear policy, anti–Vietnam War fervor, and the feminist movement. During the '80s, she became the Westchester County NOW expert on Title VII, the Equal Employment Opportunity Act, and advised women on cases of employment discrimination on the job. Her other passion during this period was working for implementation of Title IX, Equal Opportunity in Education Act, focusing on federal monies for athletic opportunities for women in school. One could say she went from hanging out to acting out to speaking out. So, although Barbara's mother was unable to give her the day-to-day nurturing she needed, nevertheless she was a good feminist role model for Barbara through her community activism and her concern for the welfare of others, which has served as an inspiration for Barbara throughout her life.

Now retired, Barbara, at 71, is busier than ever. She volunteers in two after-school reading programs, tutors children, and volunteers at the College of Mount St. Vincent Institute for Immigrant Concerns, where she assists with grant proposals, student education, and advocacy work (local and national) for new immigrants, refugees, and asylees. And, of course, she manages to throw in a good deal of political activism, too—in addition to the Granny Peace Brigade, she is active with Code Pink NYC Women for Peace and lobbies for NARAL. This is a woman who knows how to live a productive and fulfilling life beyond her official working years.

Barbara has been happily married for fifty-one years, and has two daughters, Vicki, a communications project manager, and Lesley, an attorney, and two granddaughters, Nicole and Natalie. Hats off to Barbara for conquering such difficult odds and growing up to contribute so much to others.

Bev

Beverly Rice is a perfect example of somebody who turned adversity into a positive. She was born in Greenwich Village to a 37-year-old unwed mother. "Probably the oldest first-time unwed mother ever," she says. Her mother was unable to care for her, so Bev spent her childhood in a series of foster homes and children's institutions. Perhaps as a result of this experience, during the time Bev was raising her own biological five children, she also cared for foster kids—seven in all, the last of which she adopted.

When her husband and she split up in 1970, Bev went to nursing school. She began working when her youngest child was five years old. Her first job was at Long Island Jewish Hospital where she worked in the adolescent unit. She later was employed at Memorial Sloan-Kettering Cancer Center in the bone marrow transplant division but, after three years there, left bedside nursing. "I quit because I felt like a plumber or an electrician with all those machines," she explains.

She became a corporate nurse at PaineWeber, where, in addition to her regular nursing duties, she taught CPR, held seminars, and helped coordinate the employee alcohol drug addiction rehab programs. Her intense feelings of social responsibility, however, led her back into patient care, and she went to work in an AIDS clinic in Bellevue Hospital.

Bev's second marriage was right out of a romance novel or a movie starring Audrey Hepburn. When she and her first husband married at eighteen, the service was presided over by a priest. He looked in on the growing family regularly through the years and, when Bev and her husband began having marital problems, counseled them. Eventually, he left the priesthood and got a PhD in psychology, yet he continued to check up on how Bev and her kids were doing. And, then, you guessed it, he and Bev became a couple and eventually married. They were together twenty-two years until his death in 1996, at which time she retired from nursing. Since then, she has concentrated on being a committed, and I mean *committed*, political activist and a grandmother.

Bev is very pretty and, I can testify personally, having seen her in a bathing suit, has the best body of a 70-year old woman any of us has ever seen . . . slim, flat stomach, and firm, firm, firm. And, considering she bore five children, this is most remarkable. If she weren't such a wonderful person, I could really hate her. It just isn't fair, is it?

Bev has another attribute none of us can match. She has *sixteen* grandchildren, ranging in age from 4 to 21.

Eva-Lee

Tall, commanding, and blond, Eva-Lee Baird, in addition to her striking presence, contributes a speaking voice of golden honey to the Granny Peace Brigade. When there is a dissonant clamor among us, her silken tones have an immediate calming effect.

Eva-Lee is, by any definition, an artist. She has taught animated film, video production, stage set design, painting, and drawing in schools and senior centers. She has won many awards at film festivals and student competitions for the videos she has produced with her classes. Amazingly, she has also taught mathematics, which to me is a dumbfoundingly big stretch, and has authored three books on the subject: *Going Metric the Fun Way* (Doubleday), *Nutty Number Riddles* (Doubleday) and *Science Teasers* (Harper & Row). This is clearly a woman of impressive accomplishment!

Born in New York City in 1940, Eva-Lee grew up on the Lower East Side, the habitat for so many decades of radicals, leftists, and iconoclasts of all stripes. Even though it's been gentrified quite a bit since her youth, it is still something of a stamping ground for those committed to nonconformist beliefs and lifestyles. In true Lower East Side tradition, Eva-Lee was a "Red Diaper Baby"—a child of communists. She remembers well her father telling her, over and over, that "Stalin was right and Trotsky was wrong." Eva-Lee respected her parents greatly and with burning curiosity at age 13 checked *Das Kapital* out of the library and began reading. She stopped after two hundred pages. "I didn't understand a word I read and never finished it," she says, laughing.

Because both her parents were children's book authors, they were able to escape, to some extent, the ravages of the McCarthy era, when so many people's careers were ruined through the guilt by association tactics of the House Un-American Activities Committee headed by that slimy troublemaker Senator Joseph McCarthy. According to Eva-Lee, unlike leaders in the other entertainment and arts industries, executives in the children's book field weren't concerned at all with politics, so her parents were able to sustain a livelihood, although for many years a meager one. The family of five lived in a two-and-a-half-room apartment until they left the Lower East Side when Eva-Lee was 11, moving north to the Upper West Side—coincidentally, into the same building that Granny Marie Runyon still lives in.

Like so many of the Grannies, Eva-Lee was a single mother for many years after divorcing her first husband. She has a daughter, Freedom, and a son, Noah. The unusual monicker of her daughter reflects a family habit of giving atypical names to their progeny. Her two stepbrothers, for instance, are Joseph and Karl, named after, you guessed it, Joseph Stalin and Karl Marx, not surprisingly. Eva-Lee's twin grandchildren are Karma, a girl, and Jupiter, a boy.

Scratch one of our Grannies long enough and you'll nine times out of ten come up with something truly offbeat in their history. Eva-Lee and her second husband, Dick, were married for years without living together because her building was a block and a half from her job and he had a parking space in his building. How New York can you get?

For a woman to raise two children alone while getting graduate degrees, engaging in a multiple number of complex projects with classes of teenagers, writing three books, and creating her own art is laudatory indeed, and we certainly admire Eva-Lee. Well done, woman!

Dr. Pat

We are indeed very proud to have a genuine pediatrician among us. Furthermore, Pat Salomon lives in Maryland but nevertheless traveled to New York for the purpose of participating in our action at Times Square and has joined us on other occasions, too. She is a woman of incredible commitment to causes furthering peace and justice and, as you will discover when reading her history, this dedication has underscored every aspect of her entire life.

Pat was born in 1940 in the borough of Queens and still considers herself a New Yorker despite having lived away from the city for the last twenty years. She attended Brandeis University and became friends with Abbie Hoffman, joining with him in sit-ins at Woolworth's lunch counters and other protests until she went to NYU Medical School. This was a conscious decision on her part to have a useful career and not concern herself with finding a husband to take care of her. The Cinderella Complex was definitely not part of Pat's makeup.

She felt conflicted about her medical education, which she suspected was training in professional elitism as much as medicine. Pat often had severe doubts about whether to finish. This all changed after the Mississippi Summer of 1964, when she went with the Medical Committee on Human Rights to help the Freedom Summer activities organized by the Southern Christian Leadership Council. Her job was to travel from town to town to visit the Freedom Schools, the eventual prototype for Head Start. She had to overcome a lot of fear as she moved from town to town, with black organizers crouched in the back of her vehicle so that they would escape attention. Her responsibility was to teach the moms and the schools about offering healthy food to their children, even on a limited budget. At one of the Freedom Schools, the young social activist physician met Fannie Lou Hamer, "whose dedication to improving the circumstances of her community, the deep spirituality of her presence, her wisdom and her force, the very privilege of meeting her," all changed Pat. She stopped thinking of medicine as a world; rather, it became a tool, a powerful tool, to respond in a caring way to those in need.

Care of the underserved made medicine intensely more compelling for Pat. As a pediatrician, she worked in communities where seeing a doctor was not customary; she struggled to learn Spanish to communicate better with her patients and their parents. Medicaid coverage became available during her early years of practice and families then came for care of long-neglected medical problems that were now financially possible to address. Pat says it felt wonderful to have been a part of that. Over the years of her work in community health centers, she believes she took much more than she gave. Her patients and their families had "so much to teach about struggle, endurance, and hope."

While she worked, she raised a family of six children, with the help of her loving husband, Julio, a nurse. Now grown, they continue to fill her life with love, and expand and enrich her world, as do her three grandchldren. Says Pat, "Raising a bilingual, bicultural beautiful family has been a blessing in itself. Our tribe of nuyo-jewyo-ricans is proud of their mixed heritage. We use the strengths and joys of each culture, and keep our hearts open to others."

More recently, Pat's energy has been directed at enacting a living-wage proposal in Maryland, and it just became the first state in the nation to pass a living wage. Now she is focused on getting Maryland to institute a single-payer universal health-care system, so as to focus health care on quality instead of profit. In addition, she has a foundation which deals with abused children. Pat is also devoted to the practice of yoga, for the peace and strength it gives her. For the last few years she's been studying ayurvedic medicine and last year traveled to India to learn more.

One of the most beautiful experiences of her life was watching her daughter Terry give birth to Pat's grandaughter Pilar.

Regarding her joining with the Grannies to try to enlist, Pat says, "It was easy to take on the risk of arrest, now that I was retired and my children grown. October 17, 2005, offered the special opportunity to protest with my Granny peers at the Times Square recruiting station, in an action that was both wise and humorous. The power of my age is the power to know deeply, and speak firmly about how our policies impact people's lives. As a grandmother, I can use my strength to protest with less fear and more commitment. What a privilege to have reached this place in life."

See? I told you Pat is a woman of uncommon dedication and the highest values.

Judy

Judy Lear is one of our youngest and most petite Grannies. Her bubbly personality and big brown eyes endear her to all. Judy impresses us with her courage and fortitude. She recently moved to New York by herself to begin her life anew after the shattering trauma of a husband of many years breaking up their marriage. Leaving her children, three grandchildren, and friends behind, she has forged a rewarding and active life here on her own. That takes guts.

She may look like a little doll, but she is actually a high-intellectual achiever—a Harvard grad school alumna, she is currently an adjunct professor at Fordham University as well as the leader of the Gray Panthers in New York, on their National Board and the main representative to the United Nations on their behalf. Her credits as a teacher, consultant, and organization leader are a mile long, but they just don't seem to fit with this cute little button of a woman. She is unfailingly cheerful and never confrontational, the kind of person nobody can dislike no matter how much one might disagree with her on an issue (I never do, by the way).

Judy was born, bred, and raised in Minnesota. She grew up in Minneapolis and took the giant leap across the Mississippi River to Saint Paul for her adult stint in the land of ten thousand lakes. One of the lucky ones, she says, "I had a wonderful childhood, good and loving parents, marvelous siblings (I'm the oldest of five), and was basically happy."

A misfortune occurred at age 15 when she fell off a horse and broke her hip. She was on crutches for nine months, which she says gave her a taste of what it is to be physically disabled and how people react to it. But the very next summer, she was back on horseback being a horse wrangler at a day camp!

Inasmuch as Minnesota is not too diverse, Judy always felt a bit different because she was brown eyed and had dark hair in a place where the majority were blue-eyed blonds. Also, she was Jewish in the Lutheran Land of Good People. But it didn't seem to scar her because the only anti-Semitism she remembers encountering was from a mentally disabled girl in her gym class. She was popular in high school and really enjoyed it.

She married her high school sweetheart and they were the "perfectly perfect couple." They went to the same synagogue and their parents were good friends. They grew up in the same community and their friends from high school continued in college because they all went to the University of Minnesota. Judy had three children—a daughter and two sons—all "terrific people."

She taught for two years before starting her family and then became a mom, housewife, and good spouse. Up to this point things were pretty "up" in her life. Then, in 1985, her husband fell out of love with her and into love with someone else—a typical male midlife crisis symptom. That was the end of volume 1 of Judy Lear's life and a really big downer.

Fortunately, she loved to travel and, at this difficult juncture of her life, did! A huge high point was, literally, climbing to the top of Mount Kilimanjaro in Africa (18,500 feet) and making it to the top! Another high point was getting in and actually graduating from the Kennedy School at Harvard in 1993 with a master's in public administration.

Her volume 2 has been a series of highs in traveling around the world and meeting interesting people. She says, "I've had more than my share of men and have loved every minute and each of them." She lived in Santa Fe for a while, which she says is truly "Fanta Se," and now lives in New York City. Judy adores the city and everything it has to offer.

She has realized her dreams by representing the Gray Panthers at the United Nations and being part of the peace movement. She has risen to top positions in a number of organizations—she is the North American regional chair of the International Council of Jewish Women and copresident of the Santa Fe Branch of the American Association of Uni-

versity Women. At the UN, she is the cochair of the Sub-
comittee on Older Women of the NGO Committee on the
Status of Women.

Judy's upbeat attitude toward life, no matter what kinds of
knocks she has received, is that a partially filled glass of wine
is half full, not half empty. She is a good example of how
being nurtured in a loving family environment gives one the
strength and stability to bounce back from life's blows.

Susan

Susan Asarian Nickerson is our serious painter—she's for real,
not a Sunday painter. She's a member of the National Arts
Club and the Colony Arts Center.

She attended the New School for Social Research after
getting her BA from Rutgers University and working as a social worker, then went to the Art Students League. She credits her teacher, Joseph Stapleton, with having had the greatest
influence on her work and always giving her vital encouragement. A list of her exhibitions, both solo and group, is
practically never-ending. I don't know much about the art world,
but a few places she was represented at even I have heard of:
the Broome Street Gallery, the Guild Hall Museum in East-
hampton, and the United Nations, for instance. Her paint-
ings were part of an international exhibit in China, as well.
We Grannies are very honored to have such a distinguished
artist among us.

Susan has also been a serious political activist for most of
her life, beginning in college. In more recent years, she has
been vice president and acting president of West Side Peace
Action. And, a particular project of hers has been the Ribbon
International. This is a globe-wide unique project that en-
courages the making of 36 by 18-inch ribbons sewn or painted
on fabric, showing what each individual maker loves most

and wants to protect by abolishing nuclear weapons, ending wars, and preserving the environment. Each ribbon segment celebrates the beauty and importance of life. When symbol-ically tied together, they show that the participants are ready to join with all humanity in protecting Earth's life. One such exhibition of ribbons linked together was on August 4, 1985, when over ten miles of ribbons encircled the Pentagon and other Washington, D.C., buildings. Another event occurred in 1987 in Okinawa, Japan, where such ribbons helped sur-round the largest military base in the Pacific. Nothing in the history of art compares to this enormous effort by people of many nations uniting in world support for the care and pro-tection of Earth. Our Susan is one of the directors.

She is not only a director of but United Nations non-governmental representative for the Ribbon International, and an official delegate to the Fourth World UN Conference on Women in Beijing, China, organizing televised events about the exhibit. She has traveled extensively throughout the world to fulfill her duties for the United Nations and for the Rib-bon International. She also traveled with the Granny Peace Brigade as one of six women to protest Bush in Germany and the American air bases there, in the summer of 2006.

It's hard to imagine how Susan has accomplished so much for the peace movement and yet found time to create hun-dreds and hundreds of canvases and collages *and* exhibit them—in fact, quite mind boggling.

She was born in Maine, raised there and in Florida and New Jersey. Susan's parents were Armenian refugees who es-caped to America just before the 1915 genocide, enduring many hardships and suffering extreme poverty. She speaks glowingly of her mother as a "wonderful mom and strong, compassionate woman and her greatest influence" who ar-rived in the United States as a small child unable to speak Eng-lish but went on to become a legal secretary, at times supporting her large extended family, particularly during the Depression. Susan's maternal grandmother helped many family members and friends flee Armenia and fed and clothed them when they arrived in this country. Obviously, the example of her mother's and grandmother's social activism had a strong impact on Susan, who has devoted so much of her life to the struggle for peace and justice.

Her father went through New York University on a football scholarship, but was injured at some point, leading to a heart condition he suffered throughout his life. Nevertheless, he was able to establish a business after the Depression wiped out an earlier enterprise in finance.

Susan married and had a son, Christopher Asarian, who graduated from Trinity School and the universities of Chicago and California, and is now an investment banker. (It never hurts for an artist to have an investment person in the family, I say.) After divorcing her husband, Susan had a difficult time because she was left with a half-renovated brownstone on the West Side, which she had to complete on her own— an incredibly arduous task. She was also confronted with security problems—robberies and even murders in her nice West 88th Street neighborhood. The capper occurred one day when Susan was ill and bedridden. A doctor friend had just left her home. When she heard noises emanating from another part of her house, she assumed at first that her friend had returned, but in actuality it was a young stranger. Susan had to jump out of her sickbed and chase the crook all over her house and ultimately down the street, in her nightgown. Shortly after that, she moved to the East Side (The West Side is much safer now, fully as safe as the East Side—I have to defend my turf.)

We're very lucky that Susan got arrested and jailed with us on that fateful October day in 2005, because she originally had no intention of doing so. She came to the Times

Square Recruiting Center to merely be part of the support group cheering us on, but then decided to sit down with us on the ground, leading to our visiting the hoosegow. This was definitely our gain. It was Susan who arranged, through her connection to Rev. Bob Moore of the Princeton Peace Action group, for us to receive the honor of being given the annual Patriots Award in a lovely event in Princeton during out trek to Washington in June–July 2006. She gave a most memorable acceptance speech on that occasion, which reflected our Granny group beautifully.

Jenny

It's a good thing we have a psychoanalyst among us to help smooth out the interaction chinks inevitable among a gaggle of smart and opinionated grandmothers, isn't it? Our therapist is Jenny Heinz, who has been in private practice since 1987, specializing in trauma, abuse, and dissociative disorders.

Jenny is very striking and chic, with platinum hair and hazel, almond-shaped eyes. She is fervently committed in her opposition to the war in Iraq, any possible attack on Iran, and, generally, to fighting fascism. She has good reason to be, given her amazing background as a displaced war orphan from Europe.

She was born in 1944 in Matlock, England, during the London blitz. As was the case with other pregnant women living there at that time, her mother was sent to give birth away from the constant bombing. Her mother had narrowly escaped from Austria in 1939 with her 6-year-old son and aging father, the first Jewish lawyer to teach in the University of Vienna, who had the unusual name of Achilles Rappaport. Shortly before fleeing, Jenny's mother had divorced her son's father, who escaped to Shanghai. Her brother, who was a POW in North Africa and had been captured by Rommel's forces, had met a man in the prison camp and, when the Allies liberated the camps, he sent him to seek out Jenny's mother in London. This man, who became Jenny's father, was subsequently arrested by MI5, the British intelligence agency, before Jenny was born, at which point it emerged that he had stolen the identity of a deceased English citizen and was living under an alias. Inasmuch as his real name was never known, Jenny has never been able to find out what became of him—whether he was a Nazi spy, a communist, or a Jew. The assumption is that he was deported back to Germany after being interned for years on the Isle of Man.

Her mother died when Jenny was 2 and she was sent to Summerhill, the school famous for its radical approach to raising children. Her brother, eleven years older, remained in Summerhill and later became a surgeon specializing in breast cancer, developing a procedure for postmastectomy implants. Jenny has contact with him and is especially close to his daughter, who married an American and lives in Westchester, New York.

At age 5 Jenny was brought to America by A. S. Neill, the originator of Summerhill. In the United States, she was adopted by a couple who were also refugees from Hitler and had been brought to the States in 1937 with the Salzburg Opera by the impresario Sol Hurok. They were here when Hitler invaded Austria, and never went back. Her adoptive father's older brother, who was in Switzerland with Berthold Brecht during the war, later moved to East Germany, where he became director of the East German State Theater and was awarded the Stalin Peace Prize. Her adoptive parents, as refugees, were particularly anxious during the McCarthy years and swore Jenny to secrecy not to tell any of her friends that her uncle was a big-shot communist. She, in turn, swore her best friend to secrecy and was terrified for years that her secret would be revealed.

Jenny grew up in a highly cultural and intellectual atmosphere full of music. Her father had been a tenor of note in Europe before the war, singing under the baton of Richard Strauss and also Klemperer. He studied with Busoni and was slated to study composition with Stravinsky in Paris when the war intervened. In the United States he taught at Peabody and Juilliard for many years, numbering celebrated singers among his students. A very fascinating and offbeat fact about Jenny's parents is that they were the title subjects of Oliver Sacks's book *The Man Who Mistook His Wife for a Hat*, which was later reincarnated into an opera and a film.

Jenny's mother is still alive at 103. What a contrast—a biological mother who lived to be only 42 and an adoptive one who has survived more than a hundred years!

Our therapist went only to public schools, including Hunter College High School and New York's City College. She then studied at Columbia University for a graduate degree in social work, a profession she performed within various agencies until she started her private psychotherapy practice.

We Grannies are impressed with Jenny's courage. She recently had reconstructive surgery on scar tissue caused by a bout with tongue cancer she suffered just five months before our October 17 arrest at Times Square (how's that for determination and overcoming obstacles?). Within a short time of her reconstruction work, she was back participating fully in our various activities. We only found out by default, so to speak, because Jenny seldom mentions her cancer nor ever asks for pity. A real inspiration, this one.

Jenny began her activism very early. She was only 15 when she went alone to a Woolworth's in the South to demand desegregation of lunch counters, later protested the Vietnam

War and at the Nevada nuclear test site, and right after 9/11 volunteered for thirty hours at Ground Zero. She explains her passionate struggle for peace and justice: "My origins are in wartime, where all those around me were affected by war, conquests, and the many horrors that result from dictators who attack other nations and then turn on their own citizens. I very much believe all this led me to the question that has always been my driving force: If I were a non-Jew in Nazi Germany, would I have been able to put my life on the line to save others? I question myself, because basically I consider myself a scaredy cat."

Perhaps Jenny, herself, has doubts, but all who know her have none.

Ann

One of our "Baby Grannies" (those under 65), is Ann Shirazi, who is now a first-time grandmother. Ann is also our "littlest" member, being under five feet in height. However, she is certainly one of our biggest in terms of intellect, initiative, energy, and commitment. I wonder sometimes if she's ever home except to sleep—this little dynamo is seemingly everywhere at once—protesting, demonstrating, getting arrested, creating art for our logos and banners, hosting events, traveling on behalf of the Granny Peace Brigade and other organizations. Ann is the antithesis of the expression, "There's no there there," by virtue of the fact that she's *always* there.

She was born in the Boro Park section of Brooklyn in 1945. Her father put himself through school by playing piano in the Borscht Belt, but Ann's mother said she wouldn't have her children "born in a trunk," so he left the business.

However, Ann's dad loved photography, too, and opened a photo studio in Forest Hills, but after the war the business failed. A friend had moved to Jacksonville, Florida, and wrote

that it was a "boom town" with business opportunities ga-
lore. So Ann's father transferred the family from a flat in her
grandmother's house to Florida, via train, bag and baggage,
new home unseen. Her mother went to work and Ann and
her sister became classic latchkey kids. The move to Florida
was a difficult transition and a disappointing one for her parents. They soon returned to New York, having used all their
savings. Ann was 9.

They settled in Freeport, Long Island, where she lived for
the next fifteen years. At 17, Ann went to New Paltz, a state
college specializing in art. Shortly before finals, ever the nonconformist, she was suspended from school for staying out
after curfew. She never went back but instead enrolled in the
School of Visual Arts in Manhattan, majoring in fashion il-
lustration.

In her second year there, she fell in love with an Iranian
film student, Ahmad Shirazi, from a religious Muslim family
in Tehran. Like Ann, he did not subscribe to organized religion
but had humanistic beliefs. He had come to New York to
study film at NYU and the School of Visual Arts, and planned
to take his skills back to Iran as a film director.

After graduation, Ann worked first as a sketch artist at a
buying office, and then as a newspaper artist at Arnold Con-
stable department store while freelancing for Henri Bendel.
Ahmad and she were married in her parents' backyard in
1969.

He had been hired on a New York–Iran film production,
while Ann had become Bendel's print and newspaper artist.
He wanted to return to Iran to follow his plan of becoming
a film director. At the time the couple left for Iran, however,
her mother developed neurological problems. Ann's grave
concern for her mother's condition plus working overtime on
the Bendel's Christmas catalog, coupled with the fact she had

never traveled further than the East Coast or been on an airplane, resulted in her developing an ulcer. Her new husband dragged his poor sick bride through Europe (on a far from ideal honeymoon, presumably) en route to Iran, where she lasted for less than two months before he had to bring her home to New York.

The Shirazis settled on the Upper West Side and had two sons, Arya and Nima. Ahmad became a film editor on features and documentaries, and Ann an illustrator for Abercrombie and Fitch and other stores, until advertisements began using more photography than art. In 1983, the couple created a small business, appraising old radio and television programs for donation to museums, universities and other cultural and arts institutions, which they continue to do. After leaving the fashion field, Ann spent two years as an assistant prekindergarten teacher at the Ethical Culture School. This experience had a profound effect on her and made her determined to go into social work, to specialize in child abuse cases and contribute her abilities and concerns to the larger community.

When her sons became independent, she went to graduate school and received a master's degree from Hunter School of Social Work at age 50, becoming the pediatric social worker at Lenox Hill Hospital, where she was in charge of both its in- and outpatient departments, as well as the newborn critical care unit, and trained doctors in detecting child abuse. Eventually she moved to a social service agency, Partnership with Children, serving as social work supervisor at a school on the Lower East Side, which has a sizable homeless population.

Somehow, despite Ann's full plate of motherhood, graduate school, and demanding jobs, she managed to be extremely active locally in her community and then, with the advent of George W. Bush, became a powerhouse of antiwar political activity. Among her many undertakings, she has worked with Code Pink, United for Peace and Justice, and, happily for us, the Granny Peace Brigade.

An issue very close to Ann's heart is the plight of Palestinians, and she traveled there in 2004 with Women of a Certain Age, a group of concerned women mostly over fifty, to "witness the ravages of occupation and stand in solidarity with the Palestinians against the Apartheid Wall, demolition of their homes and farmland, and destruction of their families."

Ann and Ahmad try to go to Iran every year to visit their family of 150 relatives, and a few years ago took their sons for the first time to see their family there, where "they were adored from the first moment of contact."

Although we don't always agree, this little munchkin is a much valued member of our group, always full of ideas, passion, and fresh initiatives. The graphics she has made for us are priceless; and her energy, astonishing. Here is her adorable logo for the Granny Peace Brigade, as a sterling example!

Diane

Every group has its offbeat individualist, and ours is no exception. Most of us grannies are fairly nontraditional and independent thinkers, but Diane Dreyfus, our youngest jailbird Granny, makes us look like a bunch of conformist dullards by comparison. I call her Kooky Granny sometimes, because she is so outrageously unique in a nice nutty way that I particularly appreciate. I happen to like "characters." I mean, imagine how boring life would be without them.

I first saw her at my Rockefeller Center vigil at least two years ago, although I didn't immediately know whether she was, in fact, a she or a he. All I saw was an apparition dressed head to toe as a glittering moth. The person in the costume turned out to be Diane, and was her form of protest about the environmental hazards being ignored at Ground Zero. She protested everywhere dressed like that, and was called "mothra" after the sci-fi film.

Diane has had some difficult problems in the last year or two—her marriage ended, her downtown apartment was taken over by her landlord for resale, something that is legal in New York City, unfortunately, and, at the same time, her business suffered a big downturn. As Diane puts it, "Everything went south at once." In essence, she's been an itinerant ever since—living with one of her many friends in such far-flung places as the Netherlands, Baltimore, and recently the Bronx. But Diane remains cheerful, extremely funny, and creative—writing poetry and essays, taking pictures and I don't know what all. She is a wonder . . . you could say she's averse to adversity.

Her story begins in Chicago on July 23, 1946, where she was born the daughter of an heir to the Inland Steel and Kuppenheimer Clothing fortunes. When her parents were together, they lived in Winnetka, a fancy suburb of Chicago, and in Tucson, where her dad had a mining operation, and visited Hollywood (her mother's hometown).

Diane's mother and father split, and there began a contentious custody/child support battle, involving much kidnapping back and forth of Diane and her older sister. In the midst of this tug-of-war, her father was killed in a car crash. Because he wrote the parents' wills, her uncle was able to wrest away her father's trust so that the little girls were, essentially, disinherited, given only $1,000 each. At the age of twelve, Diane was destitute. She moved to Hollywood with her mother, where she was forced to be a Nixonette, at her politically ambitious mother's bidding. This meant she had to whip off the Beatnik duds she usually wore and put on white gloves, nylons, makeup (*gasp*), and a corny little straw hat with the word "Nixonette" emblazoned on it. Her group of forty or fifty girls accompanied the President to every event he attended when in Los Angeles. This did not sit well with rebel Diane, and in her senior year at Hollywood High she began commuting to Berkeley on weekends to join protests concerning academic freedom, race relations issues, and a far-off war in Vietnam. She became a classic hippie.

While studying developmental psychology at UCLA, she began student teaching in Watts until the riots, after which she and her fellow teachers were forbidden to return. She never got to see her students again. Later at UCLA, she majored in Arabic and L.A.'s swinging nightlife. She was at an intimate party at Peter Lawford's house the night Bobby Kennedy was assassinated and was shocked at Lawford's callous reaction—talking only about taking to the funeral his then girlfriend, a Mafia princess, and the mayor of L.A., Sam Yorty, whom Diane feels didn't protect Kennedy adequately. She felt Lawford and his gang were very crass about Kennedy's death, more concerned about power and image rather than feeling genuine grief. It reminded her of her uncle's grab for her inheritance upon his brother-in-law's death. Disgusted, she hitchhiked across country, winding up in Colorado where she married her first husband . . . briefly. She spent some time in Dallas but finally landed in Columbus Circle in New York City on July 4, 1970. From there, events moved quickly in a bizarre way. Seeing no hippies, preppies, or party types, she hooked up with a guy in a yarmulke who took her to the Bronx where she got a "joe job," worked for a lawyer, and, as she puts it, "sank into the bedrock of the Bronx." Not for long. She got married again, this time to a "two-timing Persian who looked like Omar Sharif."

In brief, there were two more husbands; her own TriBeCa art gallery; a few years spent as a stockbroker ("not too successful because my sales skills were nonexistent"); the city marathon (twice); a degree in interior design and a master's in architecture; and a business of telecommunications design for trading floors. Diane thinks of herself as "the Forrest Gump of females" and, in that vein, even worked once on Cannery Row near Santa Cruz.

A close friend of Diane's, Meike, three months pregnant at the time, was visiting her from Amsterdam when disaster struck the World Trade Center. Meike remained on Diane's roof nearby for hours, photographing the mayhem despite Diane's repeated pleas to come back inside. She miscarried the following January, and her doctor was convinced it was a result of her exposure to the toxic dust of 9/11. This tragedy sparked Diane into helping to organize a 9/11 environmental action group, and she has been seriously devoted to unearthing the mistakes of the EPA and others in failing to protect the downtown environment ever since, giving a great deal of testimony regarding the Environmental Impact Statement, speaking at conferences, and the like.

Diana has no biological children of her own, but has always kept an open house for strays from Amsterdam and else-

where and figures she has had about forty "adoptees." She
honors Ernst van Aaken's concept of health: "Health must be
won and rewon daily. It is an individual's highest achievement. It is the strength of will expressed as durability." She
also honors Jonathan Schell's concept of Universal Parent-
hood, "the Fate of the Earth," and, accordingly, she coined
the term I love so much to describe our Grannies—"Universal Grandmothers."

* * *

Here, then, are the stories of the Grannies who went to
jail on October 17, 2005, all so different from one another,
with such diverse backgrounds, but united in their horror at
the direction our government was heading and by their shared
fervent desire to alter that course. ⌒

Chapter 4

Grannies in the Clink

We were taken to the hoosegow
The judge said, "Pay your bail"
We said, "We ain't payin' nohow
We'd rather stay in jail"

I've got the granny jailhouse rock blues
we're ready to pay our dues
Even when you're right, you lose
. . . That's still the news

— from the song "The Granny Jailhouse Rock Blues"

Locked Up

BEING IN JAIL wasn't exactly a new experience for some of us, actually. Bev had been in jail three times before, twice when protesting the Staten Island "nuclear port" and a third time in 2004 during the Republican Convention in New York City, where she was held for forty-six hours in filthy and deplorable conditions. Carol, Ann, and Jenny had also been arrested several times and, in some instances, did jail time. Marie had been arrested many, many times, but only once, as she recalls, actually put in a jail cell. That was in Washington, where she was arrested, along with Dr. Spock and a number of celebrities protesting nuclear arms, and placed in a jail cell with Candice Bergen.

> *"Peace requires activism, education, conversation and example. It does not come by hope or desire. We set the stage for peace and reconciliation for all children. Join us."*
> —Barbara Harris

I wasn't new to incarceration, either, having been briefly imprisoned when, like Bev Rice, I protested the Staten Island nuclear port. Inasmuch as that harbor is right smack in the middle of a confluence of the boroughs of Manhattan, Brooklyn and Staten Island, I didn't exactly cotton to the idea of hugely populous New York City being a depository for unpredictable nuclear time bombs.

The first time I was arrested, they put all of us into one big cell and left the gate partially open, so I wasn't overwhelmed by claustrophobia, my lifelong fear. Given the fact that the eminent head minister of the Church of St. John the Divine, Bishop Moore, was in the slammer with me, I felt I was in really elite company, part of the "in" crowd. The jail cell was the trendy place to be that day. It was kind of like a spontaneous party.

However, when we Grannies were locked up in October 2005, it was a bit more grim. We weren't part of an "in" crowd this time, and the gates were irrevocably and irreversibly shut. We were placed by twos in tiny, dreary cells, consisting of a hard wooden board to sit on, a toilet, and a sink. That's all, folks! We had nothing to drink, eat, or read. Our only option, and not a bad one (for a while, anyway), was that neglected pastime, conversation.

As nice as the cops had been, that's how mean the matrons of the cell block were. They treated us no differently,

I suspect, than they did their customary clientele of hookers, addicts, and petty thieves, despite the fact that we were seniors imprisoned for a peaceful political protest. When we started singing en masse from our various cells, they yelled at us rudely to shut up. When we asked for something to drink, they ignored us. I felt I was in one of those 1940s women's prison B movies, and expected any minute for the dangerous "boss" inmate to threaten me with terrible consequences if I didn't agree to give her half of all my food.

After a few hours, my cellmate, Corinne Willinger, and I were pretty much depleted of conversation. It was impossible to nap, of course, given the length and hardness of the board seat, which was just large enough for both of us to sit on. If one of us were to stretch out, the other would have to sit on the cement floor, an unappetizing prospect, given its dirt-encrusted condition. As the time dragged on, I imagined what it would be like to be incarcerated for a whole day and night, and the prospect was certainly unsettling. Corinne and I drifted into a gloomy silence.

At one point, I had the distinctly unpleasant experience of having to use the toilet in our cell, more or less for the world to see, there being no way at all of covering myself. I can't begin to describe the embarrassment and humiliation of those moments.

Two of our group were not actually placed in cells, because of their infirmities. Marie Runyon, then ninety years old, legally blind and partially deaf, was able to move around only with the help of two canes. Betty Brassell, seventy-five, used a walker. They were placed in what I suppose could be called a shape-up room—the big space where the police gathered for instructions at the beginning of their shifts and where they got snacks and drinks from vending machines. And Bev, our only jailbird nurse, was placed with them in case they needed medical attention. They were not handcuffed or

restricted and could move around the room, go to the bathroom, and use the vending machines. As Marie says now, "It
was my best arrest ever." Given the fact that Marie had
stopped counting her arrests after the twenty-eighth one, this
is indeed another example of how relatively well we were
treated by the New York cops. If only the matrons on our
cell block had followed suit.

Not all inmates were so lucky. One of the Grannies saw
a young woman prisoner being forced to stand for hours on
the cell block passageway because the jail cells were completely filled with us protesters. She noted that the girl looked
about eight months pregnant. So much for the penal system
in New York City.

Approximately four-plus hours after our incarceration, one
by one, each of us was released in turn, given an order for
a court appearance, and led to the stationhouse door. When
my turn came to emerge, a freed ex-con, I was greeted, as
were all the others, by applause from a small gathering of
supporters who had waited outside the whole time for our
liberation. I felt, again, as though I were in a movie, in this
one playing a hero being greeted by her followers after a tri-
umphant revolutionary conquest. I milked the moment to the
hilt, smiling and bowing to my constituents, before reenter-
ing my mundane life as a law-abiding citizen. It was over, or
so I thought.

Grannies Raise Hell Around the World

Even though I had done some rudimentary publicity outreach before our enlistment action, hoping it might get a little notice in a local newspaper or television program, I was
rather doubtful that it *would* get much play, given the fast pace
of breaking news 24/7 in our nonstop-action city. I needn't
have doubted.

At 7 A.M. the next morning, my phone rang, and a deep baritone voice said, "Ees zis Joan Vile?" I answered sleepily, "Yes, it is." He continued in heavily accented English, "I am Vladimir Vakanov from one of the three Russian television networks, and I would like to come to your house and interview you—now!" Fifteen minutes later, Vladimir, a tall and handsome young Russian TV anchor, and his cameraman appeared at my door and interviewed me in my pajamas. I appeared thus clad, hair tousled, eyes half shut, sans makeup, on Russian prime-time television news that very night. Thank God I have no ex-boyfriends in Russia (that I know of) to see me in such definitely non-mint condition (how mint could I be, actually, at my age?).

After they left, the phone rang continuously—an Australian radio host interviewed me by phone live on his program; NY1 News, our local round-the-clock TV news station, called and asked if I could appear that night on a show *The Call*, with any other Grannies I could round up; and other press and media calls came rushing in. Oh, to have been young again when all these attractive reporters and television newsmen started showing up in my life! I was able to get Marie Runyon to go on the NY1 show with me, and she, with her typical acerbic and witty comments, was a huge hit amongst the station's staff. In fact, the news anchor, Lewis Dodley, suggested giving Marie her own half-hour program every week to comment on the news.

The television attention was nice, but what meant the most to me was a marvelous column published in the *New York Times* that morning, again written by Clyde Haberman, the first person in the press and/or media to pay attention to us back in 2004 during one of our first vigils. Later, I Googled (yes, grannies Google, too!) "antiwar grandmothers" and saw that hundreds of newspapers and media around the world had picked up the story. We had done it—notified the world that there was a strong American opposition to the Iraq occupation and that American grandmothers were willing to go to jail to try and end it. This was one mission that *was* accomplished.

The fact that we were grandmothers made all the difference, I believe. Interestingly, Carol Husten had participated in a similar demonstration against the Iraq invasion at the same location, the Times Square Recruiting Station, before "Shock and Awe" was unleashed, except she was part of a mixed-generation group. They were jailed for eleven hours and there wasn't a single mention of their protest anywhere. I suppose one could say that being old has its occasional advantages. I'll take whatever I can get, at this point. ∼

— Chapter 5 —

Grannies Put the
War on Trial

I've got to take back my country
Find out where it went
Its principles are a mockery
And its promise has been spent
   —from the song "I've Got to Take Back My Country"

Pretrial Shenanigans

BECOMING INSTANT CELEBRITIES WAS FUN, but still the war
raged on. It wasn't morally permissible, really, for us to enjoy
too much the hoopla we aroused as long as America's grandchildren and Iraqis of all ages were dying and being maimed
every day. So, to keep the attention from going to our heads,
we pressed on with the weekly vigil. Now that we had a television, radio, and newspaper platform, we did our best to speak
cogently and stirringly of the desperate need to end the war
right away.

Two days after our arrest, we held the regular Grandmothers Against the War vigil on Fifth Avenue and were privileged to have Cindy Sheehan, America's Peace Mom, join
us. We had invited her to attend, knowing she had heard about
our arrest and wanted to support us. On that afternoon, Cindy

quietly walked over to us with no handlers, no limo or cab to transport her there, and began standing with us. She was extremely warm and gracious—she hugged us all and stayed for the entire vigil.

I'll never forget what Cindy whispered to me when we embraced each other. At this time, her son, Casey, had only been dead for approximately a year and a half. Her emotional wounds were very raw, and her words made a deep impression on me. "At first, when I found out my son had died, I wanted to die. Then, when I got involved in the struggle for peace, I found a reason to live. Now I *want* to live," Cindy said.

As a mother of two grown children, and whose daughter had a mastectomy at the age of 31 due to breast cancer, I can begin to understand the terrible agony of losing a child. My life stopped when my child was diagnosed and didn't begin again until she was pronounced well. Everything lost its meaning for me, except her health. But my daughter survived. To even contemplate her death is completely unendurable. How can any of us who haven't lost a child truly know the depths of pain a mother must experience? How do Cindy and all the other mothers who lose their kids live with this terrible tragedy? When I read occasionally that people criticize Cindy or call her an attention-seeker, I boil with anger.

None of the media attention we'd received thus far even touched the crush of reporters and cameras surrounding her. The day she came to our vigil produced the largest numbers of attendees ever—I counted sixty people. From that point on, our vigil doubled its size, except for bad weather days. Incidentally, I can't resist reporting that on days that are really inclement, especially heavy rain days, at least a few Grannies show up every time, but generally the Vets for Peace don't. Does that say anything about the stamina of women as opposed to that of the male sex? It makes one wonder where the expression "the weaker sex," comes from, doesn't it?

Grannies Go to Court

When we were released from jail, we were notified that we would have to attend a court hearing on November 15, 2005. We decided to use the occasion to try to keep our message alive to the public. But how could we intrigue the media into covering us once again, particularly inasmuch as a court appearance was far less sensational than an arrest? I decided it might be a good gimmick to buy toy handcuffs for all of us and walk to court in a single line, cuffed together. We located perfect pretend handcuffs that were practically indistinguishable from the real thing. We met a block away from the courthouse and donned the realistic-looking contraptions, cuffing ourselves together. We then slowly walked the block toward the press and media waiting in front of the courthouse. The stunt worked—that night, there we were on television news looking like ancient convicts in a chain gang.

Although our counsel, the great civil liberties lawyer Norman Siegel, made an impassioned speech to the judge in which he pleaded that we were to be honored as heroes rather than harassed with charges of disorderly conduct, the judge, a very young and probably recently appointed justice, did not dismiss our case, and we were forced to endure two more early-morning court appearances.

At our second court appearance, we waited an eternity for many other cases to be heard by the judge, wondering if we were ever to be called. Finally, one after the other, the court clerk started calling our names: "Eva-Lee Baird," "Betty Brassell," "Diane Dreyfus," until the last one, "Corinne Willinger."

We approached the bench one by one until we were all

standing together, facing the judge. As I glanced down the row—all eighteen of us standing before the bar of justice—I was overcome with emotion, and tears came to my eyes. Several others reported the same reaction. It was suddenly clear to us that we were participating in a basic struggle for the right to dissent, that we were important to the cause of maintaining our democratic principles so badly trampled on by the Bush bunch. As such, we were part of history and therefore part of the ongoing fight to preserve our Constitutional rights. The enormity and the gravity of it moved me deeply.

Some questionable tactics on the part of the prosecution became evident at the second court appearance. The assistant district attorney, one of two trying the case, a pretty blond young woman, claimed there was no videotape of the arrest action as she had said there was in a message left on Norman Siegel's phone. However, Norman pressed her on the matter, and finally she admitted that there *was* one but that she was having trouble "accessing it." We figured she was reluctant to allow it into evidence inasmuch as it would clearly show that we had not blocked entrance to the recruiting center. The judge, Alexander Jeong, commanded her to produce it at the next court hearing, but the assistant DA eventually informed Norman and the court that there was, in fact, no such videotape.

During the second appearance, we were offered the option of "adjournment in contemplation of dismissal," meaning that all charges would be dropped if we were not arrested again for six months. There was never a doubt among us about turning it down. First of all, it would have been perceived as an admission of guilt, which judgment we all firmly rejected; and second, it would have hampered our activities for too long during a time when we believed bold citizen action was essential.

At the third appearance, the judge in charge, like the two

before him, refused to dismiss our case and determined that we should stand trial before a single judge. The date was set for April 20, 2006.

Grannies Speak Their Piece

On the cold morning of April 20, 2006, I, a confirmed night person, struggled out of bed at around 6 A.M. in order to show up for our pretrial press conference at 8:30. Since I had organized the conference, I was obliged to be there on time. Somehow, I managed to do so that day and every day of the six-day trial. For me, this may have been more difficult than the four and a half hours I had spent in jail on the day we were arrested!

The Grannies assembled in the little park right across the street from the Criminal Court building in Lower Manhattan for our meeting with the press and media. Most of us were dressed in black as a symbolic mourning for our troops who had made the final sacrifice, as well as those still in harm's way in Iraq. We wore pictures of our grandchildren and great-grandchildren around our necks. Many supporters showed up, too, with their banners and signs, and we sang our unofficial anthem, our version of "God Bless America," retitled "God Help America."

The cameras and reporters were there in satisfactory numbers, and we realized we were still hot news—well, at least warm. Gosh, imagine the notoriety we would have if, in addition to

> *"Resolve all troubled relationships with the important people in your life before it's too late."*
> —Joan Wile

being ex-cons, we were involved in a sex scandal or two. Don't the people who have the biggest falls from grace occupy the biggest newspaper space?

We hustled into court for our 9:30 appearance. A huge crowd vied for seats during the proceedings, so many that the judge had to order the overflow to leave. This was most unfortunate, because it discouraged our many supporters from coming back for the balance of the trial, and, as a result, we rarely had a full house for the remaining time we were in court except for the summation and verdict on the last day.

We were worried about the judge assigned to us, Neil Ross, who had been appointed when Rudolph Giuliani was mayor. Rudy was a little conservative for our tastes, and we figured any appointee of his to the court would be a stickler for the most picayune parts of the law. Judge Ross was young enough to be our son, about 46, rotund, and with a loud, commanding voice. He projected an aura of no nonsense yet had a good sense of humor, and we were quite amused by him some of the time.

Norman and his cocounsel, Earl Ward, a handsome young attorney with experience in criminal defense law, had told us that they would try to put every one of us on the witness stand and thereby turn the tables on the establishment and put the *war* on trial rather than us. All eighteen of the Grannies were there and each prepared to testify concerning the reasons for her participation in the action.

Norman's plan worked—far beyond expectations. After the prosecution presented their laughably inadequate and conflicting testimony, during which the various policemen who arrested us contradicted each other blatantly as to the details of the incident, a succession of Grannies was put on the witness stand. Norman and Earl asked every one of us why we engaged in the action we did, and every Granny expressed her opposition to the war and her desire to replace the young

The rally that started it all: Barbara Barrie speaks at the first Grandmothers Against the War rally at the Eleanor Roosevelt statue in Riverside Park in Manhattan, November 2003. PHOTO: JOAN WILE

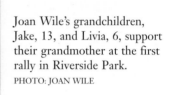

Joan Wile's grandchildren, Jake, 13, and Livia, 6, support their grandmother at the first rally in Riverside Park.
PHOTO: JOAN WILE

The New York Granny Chicks perform at Holy Name Church, January 2005, *from left to right:* Helen Miles, Joan Wile, and RoseMarie Jun.
PHOTO: HAL MILES

The Grandmothers Against the War hold a vigil every Wednesday on Fifth Avenue near Rockefeller Center, here Joan Wile (*third from left*) and Judy Goldstein. PHOTO: MARK MANLEY

Activist Cindy Sheehan, in a show of support for the Grandmothers Against the War, joins Joan Wile at the Rockefeller Center vigil just two days after the grandmothers' arrest in Times Square, October 2005. PHOTO: BETTY BRASSELL

Granny Peace Brigade member Beverly Rice, in her home. PHOTO: MARK MANLEY

Granny strategy session at the War Resisters League offices, January 2006; *from left to right:* Carol Husten, Lillian Rydell, (unidentified), Barbara Walker, Molly Klopot, and Beverly Rice. PHOTO: MARK MANLEY

The Grannies, led by Betty Brassell and Norman Siegel, file into criminal court for their trial, April 2006. PHOTO: MARK MANLEY

Grannies listen to attorney Norman Siegel before their April 2006 trial; *left to right:* Susan Nickerson, Marie Runyon and Siegel. PHOTO: MARK MANLEY

Molly Klopot, and Barbara Walker, and other Granny Peace Brigade members and supporters with Norman Siegel before heading into court. PHOTO: MARK MANLEY

The Granny Peace Brigade gathers at the Times Square demonstration, Valentine's Day, 2006; *left to right:* Barbara Harris, Betty Brassell, Barbara Walker, Molly Klopot, Joan Wile, Ann Shirazi, Eva-Lee Baird, and Jenny Heinz. PHOTO: HERB HECSH

Sue Niederer, whose son was killed in Iraq, tried to enlist in the U.S. Army on Valentine's Day, 2006, in Times Square. She wasn't able to enlist, but she was able to join the Granny Peace Brigade in their demonstration. PHOTO: JOAN WILE

The Raging Grannies perform at the Valentine's Day demonstration, February 2006. PHOTO: MARK MANLEY

German hosts await members of the Granny Peace Brigade at the Berlin Airport, March 2006, *left to right:* Fritz Neumann, Reverend Peter Kranz, Elisabeth Kranz, and fellow host. PHOTO: BARBARA WALKER

Marie Runyon outside Criminal Court after a hearing, March 2006. PHOTO: MARK MANLEY

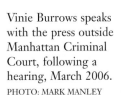

Vinie Burrows speaks with the press outside Manhattan Criminal Court, following a hearing, March 2006. PHOTO: MARK MANLEY

Carol Husten impersonates
Barbara Bush at the Granny
Cabaret at St. Luke's Church,
December 2006.
PHOTO: HERB HECSH

The Granny Cabaret performs at St. Luke's Church, December 2006, *left to right:*
Barbara Harris, Barbara Walker, Jenny Heinz, Ann Shirazi, Judy Lear, and Joan Wile.
PHOTO: HERB HECSH

Grandmothers Against
the War member Betty
Brassell at the weekly
Rockefeller Center vigil.
PHOTO: MARK MANLEY

Barbara Walker makes a point at the weekly Grandmothers Against the War Rockefeller Center vigil. PHOTO: MARK MANLEY

A Granny wearing a photo of one of her grandchildren at the weekly Rockefeller Center vigil. PHOTO: MARK MANLEY

Joan Wile at a Grandmothers Against the War
demonstration, 2006. PHOTO: MARK MANLEY

The Granny Peace Brigade gathers at the Endless War Memorial in Times Square,
March 2007. PHOTO: DIANE DREYFUS

people losing their lives, their limbs, and their sanity in an immoral and illegal war based on lies. Each of us explained that we had been blessed with long and productive lives and were willing to put ourselves in harm's way so that the young soldiers could come home and have the same opportunity for full life spans as we had enjoyed.

Each grandmother was eloquent in her individual way. Dr. Patricia Salomon stated: "I was exercising my First Amendment right, especially since Congress is doing nothing about the war. Young people should not waste their lives in war. I have seen too many burned bodies of young people in this war."

"We are at a very important point in the history of our country," 87-year-old Molly Klopot said. "It is our responsibility as patriots not to be silent."

Carol Husten said: "I love my country, but I need to express my opinion as part of my First Amendment right. This country has become a military industrial complex, which is exactly what President Eisenhower warned us about as he left office, and I must sound the alarm bell."

And leave it to our outrageous character, 90-year-old Marie Runyon, to state her case with her characteristic, shall we say, candor: "We did it to tell that son of a bitch in the White House to *stop* it!"

Frank Barbaro, a New York State assemblyman for over twenty years and a recent criminal court judge, came from his home in Albany to testify on our behalf. We had asked him to observe our action at Times Square, which he willingly did, and he was thus able to testify that we had left space for people to pass through into the recruiting center. It was a definite plus for us. Who could dispute the word of a criminal court judge?

After we had all testified, which took up a good two days, the time came for Norman Siegel's summation. It was so stirring, there was complete silence as Norman addressed the courtroom, his voice impassioned and confident:

> These eighteen defendants are people of conscience. On October 17, 2005, they acted on principle in the great American tradition of peaceful, nonviolent protest. They walked in the shoes of great Americans who have made this nation and city as great as we are. We are a better society and a better city because of citizens who stand up, speak out, and visibly and vocally are prepared when other means fail, to even get arrested, to bring needed public attention to their underlying grievance.

We were told by Judge Ross to take an hour's break, after which we were informed the verdict would be handed down. We knew that if we were found guilty we could be required to pay a fine, do community service, or even serve a jail term for up to fifteen days. We waited on tenterhooks to learn our fate.

After that hour, we filed in to our seats in the jury boxes. Because there was no jury, and some of the grannies were hard of hearing, the judge kindly allowed us all to sit near him in what would normally be the jury chairs. Judge Ross then recited his verdict:

> Consequently, having considered all of the evidence in this case and applying all of the appropriate legal principles, I find that the People have failed to prove each individual defendant guilty of each count beyond a reasonable doubt, and therefore I find the defendants not guilty. The defendants are all discharged.

We left the courtroom in a state of euphoria, and were greeted by a crush of reporters and supporters, indeed causing us to feel for the moment like heroines. I now have an appreciation of how Rocky must have felt when he won his impossible victory.

Norman Siegel spoke to us outside the courthouse after the verdict. He said, "The decision today says the First Amendment protects you to protest peacefully." Smiling broadly, he added, "So—go do it!"

Which is exactly what we did. ⌒

Chapter 6

Bolt the Doors! The Grannies Are Coming!

Oh, they gave us the Patriot Act
Watch our rights dribble down the tubes
See our Constitution attacked
Let's keep pestering those arrogant boobs
　　—from the song "Grannies, Let's Unite"

DURING THE TIME PERIOD LEADING UP TO OUR TRIAL, the group of women who had been arrested wanted a name to identify it separately from Grandmothers Against the War, so we jailbirds became the Granny Peace Brigade. Now we felt it was important to capitalize on the fact that we were in the public eye and continue our antiwar activities. We wondered what our next step should be. The answer came in January when a woman in Berkeley, California, Marge Lasky, e-mailed me that she had heard of our October arrest action and, inspired by us, had started a group of her own, the Bay Area Grandmothers Against the War. She wanted to initiate a nationwide grandmothers' action for Valentine's Day, duplicating our attempt to enlist at recruiting centers, and asked if I could help. I loved the idea and contacted Granny groups in other cities to see if it could be pulled together. Through our connections with Code Pink, Grandmothers for Peace International, and others, we managed, along with the Bay Area group, to get activists in sixteen different cities to agree to go along with the plan.

Our local Granny Peace Brigade group had a few stormy sessions about how we should participate. Some insisted that we should do as we had before—try to enlist and risk getting arrested again. Others, including me, were reluctant. I felt that a second arrest so soon after the first was too chancy, especially considering we had a trial coming up, and that if we did get any coverage it would seem like rehashed news.

A flash idea attacked me, utterly outrageous, really. Instead of holding what would probably amount to another sit-in, it occurred to me that maybe we should dance at the Times Square recruiting center. After all, the center was located right in the heart of Broadway, so it was more than appropriate that we should put on a show there. I suggested hesitantly at our next meeting that we perform a chorus line at the recruiting center on Valentine's Day. I thought I would be laughed out of the room but, to my surprise, the Grannies went for it, and it was decided that we'd dance instead of trying again to enlist.

But first we had to find somebody to choreograph a routine for us. I turned to one of the very first vigilers, Marjorie Perces, an old friend with a very impressive résumé as a dancer, choreographer, and teacher (she taught Alvin Ailey, as a matter of fact). Marjorie was now about 82 but still quite limber, and she agreed to be our choreographer.

About ten of us went to her little studio and tried to perform the steps she gave us, but they were very difficult for us old dames, involving a lot of lying down on the floor and then the impossible part—getting up. As we had learned when we did our Times Square action, our worn bodies were hardly in condition for this kind of punishment, and besides, as we gracelessly catapulted to the floor we looked more like a bunch of lumbering hippopotamuses than swans. We didn't see the connection of lying on the ground to our antiwar image. Further, she wanted us to pass a bottle of water down the line and each drink quickly from it. We worried that any observers there might be wouldn't know if it was water or demon alcohol. When the rehearsal ended, we discussed it in Marjorie's building lobby (without her, tactfully) and agreed it wouldn't work for us. I was very worried about how to break the news to Marjorie and agonized about it for a few days. Finally, I gathered up my courage and told her. To my surprise and relief, she took it very well, almost dismissively.

There was very little time left at that point before Valentine's Day, and in desperation I turned to a very dear friend of mine, who, coincidentally, had been a student of Marjorie's—Barry Martin.

I had met Barry about fifteen years earlier after reading a story about him in *People* magazine. He had once been a talented dancer, who, at 21, got his first job as a principal with a prestigious British group, Hot Gossip. They began touring Africa, and one of their stopping-off places was Sun City, South Africa, supposedly untainted by apartheid. Barry was assured that he, a black man, would be safe there.

Shortly into the tour, Barry was in an automobile accident in Sun City. The car was driven by one of the white male dancers. An ambulance came and carried the white young man away and left Barry on the road. He assumed he must not have been as badly injured as his friend, for why else, he wondered, would they abandon him at the accident scene. Eventually, some people came along and took him to a nearby hospital. He remembered that he was able to walk in, with help. However, he was not admitted because of his skin color,

> *"surprize yourself*
> *don't make it up in advance*
> *it is what it is*
> *paying attention is an act of love*
> *if you are coming from a kind place*
> *you can say anything that comes to mind.*
> *improvisation is the key to success*
> *study forever*
> *no one can take your knowledge*
> *and you will have lots to give away"*
> **—Diane Dreyfus**

and was driven seventy-five miles over rough roads to another hospital. His neck, which was broken, was not secured, so that by the time he arrived at the next hospital, his spinal cord was severed and he was a quadriplegic, doomed never to dance again.

After a year of rehab in a British facility, he was sent back to his home in Queens, New York. When I read his story in *People*, my heart broke. I wrote him a letter of encouragement in care of the magazine, never expecting it would actually get through to him. Two weeks later, I received a call from Barry, who had gotten my letter, thus beginning an extraordinary friendship with the most remarkable person I've ever known.

Before I met him, upon his return to New York, Barry had entered a master's program in arts administration at New York University, and as part of his thesis project put together a dance company which he called Deja Vu Dance Theater.

He developed a technique whereby he drew rudimentary stick figures with a pencil attached to his fingers. He had retained a modicum of gross motor movement in his shoulders and was thus able to propel his hand and create these amazingly realistic drawings of dance moves. With this tool plus his verbal instructions to the dancers, he created beautiful works that were performed at Lincoln Center, Town Hall, and many other venues.

He invited me to one of his early performances. When I saw this beautiful young man sitting motionless in his wheelchair in the rear of the theater, my heart went out to him for keeps. We got closer and closer—he called me his second mother, and I referred to him as my second son (my biological son is two months older than Barry). I began helping him raise money for his dance group and undertook some other tasks on his behalf.

In all the years I knew Barry, I never heard him complain nor did I ever see him exhibit bitterness. He was always upbeat, and always helpful to his friends and family. Many times I went to Barry with an artistic problem, and he always came up with a valuable suggestion or two. During the course of his life after his accident, he did a number of things—wrote a movie script, advocated for access of the disabled to theaters, created a play based on his life, had a part on a *Law & Order* episode on television, and, most amazingly of all, became a substitute teacher in public schools in New York (can you imagine that?), all this in addition to choreographing and administrating a dance company. Barry was quite simply the absolutely best person I've ever known. I truly loved him.

So, I asked Barry to help us put together a dance for Valentine's Day, even though I knew he was very busy with his new project, creating a children's dance theater. As so typical of Barry, he didn't hesitate to say yes. There wasn't much time—about two weeks until February 14. He hired a rehearsal studio, and about eleven or so Grannies showed up. We spent two hours with Barry and he shaped a dance for us. The Grannies all adored him, and we looked forward to the next rehearsal in a few days. But, before the rehearsal, just three days after we had worked with him, his mother called to tell me he had died—at the age of 44. His death is a mystery—it seems the aide assigned to him for that twelve-hour period (he always had aides 24/7) did not complete his shift and left Barry alone. Apparently, Barry had some sort of attack and wasn't able to get help. He was found the next morning in his wheelchair by the inside of the front door of his apartment.

The Grannies were devastated, but we did our best to reconstruct the dance moves Barry had created for us.

Valentine's Day 2006 was very cold, and a snowstorm had left New York's streets and sidewalks covered with a treacherous icy glaze. The recruiting center doors were closed, and if there were people inside, we knew they would not acknowledge our presence. The little traffic island at the site of the recruiting booth was totally covered with ice, making it extremely dangerous for us to try to dance. However, Jenny Heinz had the clever idea of searching for sand, which she, by some miracle, found, and which she then spread over an area big enough for us to perform. Somebody else, by cell phone, located a city agency which sent a person to scrape off the ice. There weren't many people to witness this incident, but a few hardy souls showed up, along with a few cameras and reporters. We had no microphones, and this fact plus the ear-splitting Times Square traffic made it a bit difficult for us to be heard. But we pressed on nevertheless. After all, we were the Granny Peace Brigade, and nothing stopped us from our appointed rounds!

Our beloved defense attorney, Norman Siegel, acting as master of ceremonies, made a short speech about our goals and actions, after which we proceeded with our unique production.

We were very intent on getting every detail right, not only so as to perform well, but to honor the memory of Barry. Taking our courage in hand, we did the dance, high kicks and wiggling hips, while singing our version of "There's No Business Like Show Business," retitled and with new lyrics, "There's No Business Like War Business," and then changing pace and moving slowly while we sang "Where Have All the Flowers Gone?" We even had a homemade full-size cardboard coffin covered with the American flag as a backdrop and put real flowers on it as we ended the dance. I don't know how it happened, or, rather, *didn't* happen, that nobody slipped and fell.

Next in the line-up, I sang my song, "Grannies, Let's Unite." I had started writing songs about our Granny doings shortly after I formed Grandmothers Against the War and had organized a trio I called the New York Granny Chicks with two of my old studio singing colleagues, Helen Miles and Rosie Jun. We had begun performing at peace meetings, campaign events, and for THAW (Theatres Against War) Freedom Follies shows in theaters, and became sort of darlings of the peace circuit. I didn't anticipate it at the time, but this performance sideline gradually lengthened into a full Granny cabaret show, the chorus line dance being the second act added on.

After my song, Vinie Burrows, our actress Granny, gave a powerful dramatic reading. For the record, Vinie's Broadway debut, at the age of 15, was with Helen Hayes in *The Wisteria Trees.*

At that point, Carol Husten did the most gutsy thing of

all. At the age of 74, she made her debut as a stand-up comedienne. Dressed in a blue suit, with big pearls, and adorned
by a huge white fright wig, she did a comedy routine im-
personating Barbara Bush. I've performed a thousand times
in public singing, playing instruments, and occasionally acting, but never would I have had the sheer guts it takes to do
comedy . . . alone. I have to bow to Carol for doing something so scary, and doing it so well. She has done it many
times since, always with updated material relative to the current news, and the audiences love her.

Following the show, Gold Star Mother Sue Niederer gave
a stirring and moving talk about the death of her son, Seth,
in Iraq two years previous. At the end of her speech, Sue attempted to go inside the recruiting station to enlist, but the
recruiters inside locked the doors when she approached and
she was unable to enter the facility. Perhaps they were nervous about the huge signs she wore on her front and back,
which had the words "George Bush killed my son" inscribed
on them, as had her T-shirt when she attended a meeting
held by Laura Bush at the 2004 Republican Convention. At
that time, she was dragged out in handcuffs. This is America in the twenty-first century, folks.

At the end of the action, we dispensed little chocolate hearts
to all the onlookers and then we Grannies and our followers marched almost a mile to the offices of senators Hillary
Clinton and Chuck Schumer, both of whom had been supporters of the Iraq occupation. The grandmothers were unable to go inside the senators' office buildings, but gave a bill
of particulars for immediate withdrawal of troops in Iraq to
staff members who came outside.

Exhausted, we called it a day. All in all, fifteen other cities
had actions simultaneous with ours, with some grandmothers
getting arrested and a few doing jail time. Some of them got

excellent press coverage, thereby further spreading the anti-war word. We got minimum coverage, ourselves, but felt it had been a very worthwhile action overall, with so many cities learning about grannies' determination to end the war. We had successfully gone national! ∼

— *Chapter 7* —

Grannies Go to Berlin

I'll keep on keeping on
No, I won't be silent
So when I'm dead and gone
the world will know where I went
—from the song "I'll Keep on Keeping On"

AFTER MONTHS OF ACTIVITY, Grandmothers Against the
War had gone national. Little did we know we were shortly
to become *international*! Word of our little group had already
begun to spread beyond the borders of the United States.
Early in our vigil, a woman walked by one day and wrote an
article for a popular French daily. As already mentioned, a
young Japanese producer for Japanese National Television
created a documentary about us, which stirred a few other
Japanese peaceniks to drop by our vigil when they were in
New York, and a few articles about us were published in the
Japanese press. In fact, I believe Japan and Germany were
our most enthusiastic fans. We've also had excellent press and
media exposure in Russia. I find it ironic that we received
our biggest coverage in the three countries that had been our
principal enemies in the past, although I was never one to
feel hostile to Russia. It says something about the futility of
war, doesn't it?

In March, shortly before our trial was to begin, I got an

e-mail from a Rev. Peter Kranz, inviting me to speak in Berlin to several church peace groups. Cindy Sheehan was originally slated to speak, but she canceled a projected tour of Europe and was therefore unable to keep her commitment in Germany.

This presented me with a real personal dilemma. I had fear of flying. I'd promised myself never to fly again years and years ago, and was able to stick to my vow except for a trip about seven years earlier to visit my daughter and grandchildren when they briefly lived in California. In 1989, I had even figured out a scheme to go all the way to Russia and back without flying—by ship and train. It was an incredible journey, principally because I met the wonderful people our government for so long had determined were our enemies. But, the thought of *flying* overseas? Of *flying* across the Atlantic Ocean? No, thank you. Unthinkable!

But I couldn't stop ruminating on it. I realized how important it was to let people in other countries know that there was an opposition to Bush's war, to try to restore at least a little our damaged reputation around the world, and here was the perfect opportunity. I kept thinking there was no way I could do it, but finally I decided that there was no way I *couldn't* do it. I asked Rev. Kranz if I could bring a couple of other Granny Peace Brigade jailbirds with me, and he agreed. I certainly had no intention of going alone!

Barbara Walker and eighty-seven-year-old Molly Klopot, chair of the New York Chapter of the Women's International League for Peace and Freedom, the oldest international women's peace and justice group, volunteered to go with me. With great trepidation, and with a modest ingestion of Xanax, I boarded a Delta jet with my companions in the evening of March 16 and anxiously took my seat, consciously selected to be well away from the windows so I couldn't see how far we were from the ground below. As you can surmise, I survived the flight.

In fact, I began to relax during the trip and was even able to look out a window several times.

We arrived in Berlin the next morning and were greeted by the nicest group of people one could ever expect to know. I had some negative feelings about Germans, left over from having been a child during World War II disposed to hate them, and also because I am three-quarters Jewish. But all such feelings were dispelled once I was in the warm company of these wonderful people. Rev. Peter Kranz, head minister of the Luther Church Spandau-Berlin, his wife, Elisabeth, and their friends, showed us the hospitality that Germans are famous for—and then some.

We were housed in Peter and Elisabeth's roomy and comfortable apartment in Spandau, a sort of borough of Berlin. It appeared to be a middle-class neighborhood, quiet and conventional. We were surprised to learn that because of a severe unemployment condition, a number of alcoholic men would sprawl about the streets near the church most mornings.

We were fed exquisite meals prepared by Elisabeth. Breakfast, for instance, always provided tasty homemade breads and muffins, as well as an assortment of cheeses, eggs, and cereals. Their friend, Fritz, carted us around in his car, and he and his wife, Elke, hosted a lunch for us featuring a terrific lentil soup with sausage.

That first night, each of us spoke to Peter's congregation,

> *"Activism is great for the juices. When we feel more alive, and have more purpose and meaning in our lives, we are definitely more sexy."*
> **—Dr. Pat Salomon**

St. Nikolai Kirche in Berlin-Spandau, a lovely Gothic church
that is one of the oldest in Berlin; and I sang a couple of my
granny antiwar songs. Peter had arranged for a translator, so
we were able to communicate adequately to those who didn't
speak English. On the program with us at all meetings we
attended was a young American, David LaMotte, a fine speaker
and excellent guitarist-singer who performed, with his percus-
sionist friend, Chris Williams, some of David's original works.

The next day, Peter and his friends took the three of us
on a tour of Berlin that was so fascinating as to make the
trip worthwhile for that alone. We went through the Bran-
denberg Gate to the part of the city that had been East Berlin
during its partition phase and strolled on the legendary wide
boulevard, the Unter den Linden. We were amazed to see beautifully reconstructed landmarks—the Hotel Adlon, Humboldt
University, and the Berliner Dom. We went into the Reichstag
and climbed to the top to the viewing platform so we could
see the city surrounding us. Everywhere we went beyond the
gate were beautiful buildings and well-maintained parks. East
Berlin, once drab and poverty stricken before the Wall came
down, was now the showcase of the metropolis and considered
the better section, contrasted with the former West Germany.

We also were taken to a remarkable museum, the Citadel
Spandau, in a former castle and medieval fortress, which, in
an exhibit entitled "Berlin 1945," displayed photos of Berlin
from before the beginning of the war to the aftermath. The
museum was endlessly long, and there were hundreds of pho-
tographs, openly showing the terrible destruction of the city.
Among many of the very interesting photos were several of
the *Trümmerfrauen*, the so-called Rubble Women, who ardu-
ously gathered, brick by brick and mortar by mortar, all the
debris from the bombed-out buildings of Germany, which was
then used to rebuild. They were assigned this task because

so many of the German men had died or were still in Allied prisons. I thought a brief section concerning the Holocaust rather scanty in its lack of depth and sufficient coverage, but the fact it was displayed at all was, I suppose, something to be grateful for.

We gave two more presentations with songs to Peter's church and to Heilands, a church beautifully reconstructed from ruins in an octagonal shape with stunning stained glass windows. We were always met with an enthusiastic response. People crowded eagerly around us after we finished, their faces shining with warmth and approval. Those who could speak English were happy to hear Americans voice opposition to the war in Iraq. It was a real love fest. Audiences particularly loved Molly for her energy and articulateness, so unexpected in a woman of her advanced years. Molly had lived in Berlin for a while shortly after the war ended, as had Barbara at a later date—in both cases on a work assignment.

Sightseeing and visiting aside, it was also very interesting to watch the international version of CNN. Generally, the international CNN reportage seemed far more extensive and impartial than what was fed to us in the United States. We were pleasantly surprised to see a piece about ourselves demonstrating at one of the vigils, which we hadn't seen at home.

Our four days in Berlin were delightful, and we returned home with great sadness at leaving behind such good people that we feared we might never see again. In addition to carrying on their local ministry and expressing their strong opposition to the war in Iraq, Peter and Elisabeth spend time in El Salvador assisting people there. As Molly said, "They live their religion."

The flight back was uneventful, and some of my phobia was eased. But would I fly again? Sorry to say, probably not.

This trip helped ameliorate my fear somewhat, but did not cure it.

As short as our trip was, we felt that we had helped bridge the painful gap in our relationships with the rest of the world created by our administration's policies and hoped we had been instrumental, in our small way, in healing the breach.

— Chapter 8 —

Grannies Take Their Show on the Road

I'll keep on keeping on
No matter what the cost
I'll keep on keeping on
Before our rights are lost
    —from the song "I'll Keep on Keeping On"

Tax Day

WE WERE NOW SO MUCH IN THE PUBLIC EYE that, in order to spread our message ever more widely, we felt a definite pressure to remain in the headlines. Our next opportunity to stage a significant event that we hoped might attract media attention came on Tax Day, Monday, April 17, 2006.

We again created a nationwide grandmothers action, and were able to pull together about twelve groups from various locales: Essex County, New Jersey; East Palo Alto; Madison, Wisconsin; Detroit; Manhattan; Harlem; Sacramento; Bellington, Washington; Philadelphia; Pittsburgh; Sierra Foothills; and Tucson.

You will note that we had a Harlem Grandmothers Against the War group among our participants. This made us very happy, as we had been hoping for a long time to make the grandmothers antiwar movement more reflective of the general population. Vinie Burrows went to work and contacted her friend, Bill Perkins, a former New York City councilman from the Harlem district (and currently representing his area in the New York State Senate). Bill was a particular favorite of the Grannies for his outspoken and consistent opposition to the war in Iraq while on the council, and also for his support of us. Some of us attended hearings he held in the City Council in an effort to have New York City sign on to the Peace Tax Bill. He was able to bring together a number of Harlem Grannies for our Tax Day event.

The various groups of Grannies across the country went to IRS offices and recruiting centers and sang and chanted and distributed literature, and I believe a few tried our old tactic, attempting to enlist. Some got a fair amount of coverage in the press and media. Those of us in New York carried out a two-pronged approach, in which some of the Grandmothers went to the big midtown Manhattan General Post Office and distributed fliers with pie charts detailing the obscene huge portion of the United States budget that went to the war machine, and, conversely, the equally obscene tiny portion that went to our basic needs—education, health care, housing, and the like. Others held a rally on Harlem's legendary 125th Street in front of the IRS office there, which, conveniently for us, was located directly across the street from the local recruiting center. Bill Perkins and other local politicos orated, and our dynamic Vinie Burrows gave one of her stunning speeches. Vinie is extraordinarily gifted at conjuring spontaneous remarks on any subject. She can do this on a dime and always mesmerizes audiences, so we generally have her be the spokesperson for us at rallies and interviews. She is our best foot forward. Her speech that day contained the following: "The war in Iraq translates itself into a war on the poor, particularly right here in Harlem and the other

Harlems in this nation, the barrios and the Indian reservations of the United States. We are paying a heavy price, a deadly price, for the war in Iraq."

We had now engaged in several noteworthy antiwar actions—our arrest, the trial, our national Valentine's Day and Tax Day protests, and our Berlin trip. In addition, the New York Granny Chicks, my vocal trio, continued to perform for various progressive-oriented occasions, including two years performing on Martin Luther King Jr. Day at Holy Name Church, an enormous Catholic Church on the Upper West Side. We were invited to do so by Father Mike Tyson—*not* the boxer, I hasten to assure you. Father Mike is a Franciscan monk, an outspoken critic of the war who annually organizes a peace march on MLK Day, during which West Siders walk with him from church to temple to church throughout the area prior to a mass at Holy Name (at which we sang). At one of his events, we were honored to appear with Father Daniel Berrigan, the great anti–Vietnam War leader. All these things, to greater or lesser degree, were made known to the public through newspapers, radio and television interviews, and some word of mouth.

But still the war raged on.

The death toll of American service people kept rising. Iraqis were being attacked in increasingly horrible ways. We felt a desperate need to do more. We Grannies searched for a new exploit that would have further-reaching impact. Norman Siegel came up with the idea of our going on a trek from New York to Washington to spread the word and inspire and encourage others to take more aggressive action to stop the war.

Ye gods! A *trek* from New York through cities and towns all the way to Washington, stopping everywhere along the way to speak, to perform, to interact? I didn't know whether to thank Norman or curse him! Organizing the trek involved complicated arrangements: unearthing generous people in approximately twelve cities and towns to provide accommodations for approximately twenty-five Grannies, plus a film crew assigned to do a documentary about our trek; arranging for events where we could speak to the public; concocting a feasible travel route; and endless other details to be worked out. To say nothing of the need to raise thousands of dollars quickly to cover expenses!

The Trek

We worked out all the complex arrangements and raised the necessary $10,000-plus in, amazingly, about six weeks. It was decided that we would launch our trek on Saturday, June 24, and end in Washington on July 4. We rented a Greyhound bus to cart us long distances between cities but, wherever possible, we planned to walk within the places we visited.

Our mission statement, which we announced at our opening day press conference and included in all our press releases, read as follows:

> Our purpose is to show that Granny Power is a force to be reckoned with. We intend to demonstrate that the people are rising up to defeat the catastrophic policies of the Bush administration. We intend to prove that older people have a vital role to play in life, and that we must. We intend to bring our young people home from Iraq in one piece. We intend to take back our country.

The night before the trip, most of us slept little and fretted mightily about our historic adventure. How would a group of seniors (aged 59½ to 91) cope with what promised to be an exciting but arduous journey? The weather forecast was foreboding at best, predicting downpours and thunderstorms throughout the first day of the trek.

Day 1: A Drenching Downpour

On the morning of June 24, 2006, sixteen of the original eighteen-member Granny Peace Brigade plus a few supporters gathered to begin our peace trek to Washington, D.C. I was up at six A.M. after only about four hours of sleep. I called the press and media one last time in my attempt, as unofficial publicist for the Grannies, to urge them to cover our send-off. A few young men loaded with camera equipment burst into my apartment to shoot my preparations for the trek. They were part of the film crew for the documentary that Bob Sann and his wife, Fran Sears, were going to produce about us. A camera practically stared down my throat as I ate my cantaloupe and it was all I could do to keep the device from accompanying me to the bathroom. I began to think that maybe being a movie star had its negative aspects but, on the other hand, at my age it's quite gratifying to have so such close attention, I must admit.

I arrived at Columbus Circle, where the other Grannies were assembling for the beginning of our walk. We loaded our things onto the bus and, since it was already beginning to rain, resignedly donned ponchos and raincoats and opened our umbrellas, determined to withstand the elements and walk the sixteen blocks down to the scene of our noncrime at the Times Square recruiting center, the official starting point of our trek. In addition to our own documentary film crew, a CNN camera crew, a Japanese TV network camera crew, and assorted photographers tagged along with us, so that it appeared there were nearly as many cameras as grannies bobbling along in the rain down Broadway.

By the time we reached the recruiting center island, it was pouring! Undaunted, we proceeded with our press conference. Our attorney, Norman Siegel, began the proceedings with an inspired statement about the purpose of our trek, fol-

lowed by Congressman Charles Rangel; our pal State Senator Bill Perkins; national cochair of United for Peace and
Justice Leslie Cagan; Reverend Billy of the Church of Stop
Shopping; Air America radio talk host Mark Riley (who invited us to call in each morning of the trek to report our
progress, which we did), and other notables. I was particularly gratified that actress Barbara Barrie again came to support the Grannies and spoke eloquently to the cameras. Barbara
is a firmly committed antiwar grandmother herself, and she
offered to help that day despite a very tight schedule.

The rains came harder and harder, but we "stayed the
course," in the words of Shrub's endlessly recited directive
for resolving our catastrophic crisis in Iraq (thank you, Molly
Ivins, for that marvelous nickname for the present resident
of the White House). We persevered through the hours-long
press conference in the middle of waterlogged Times Square.
Oh, did I mention the relentless heat and humidity? Even
the raindrops did nothing to mitigate it.

After the press conference concluded, we climbed onto our
nice, dry, and air-conditioned bus for a ride to the Brooklyn
Bridge, which we planned to cross on foot. Much to our dis-
may, a terrible drenching downpour had occurred shortly before we were scheduled to cross the bridge, prompting many
of us to worry and give up hope. "Forget it, we can't do it . . .
we'll be drowned, we'll slip on the wet wooden walkway—
no way!" But the bus driver's 13-year-old son, Zack Bern-
stein, our escort and official mascot for the trip, said: "You
have to go. You've told the world you're going to do it, and
you can't back off now. If you do, then people will think
you're weak in your commitment." As the saying goes, "A
little child shall lead them." We all filed off the bus and
walked across the magnificent bridge, in a cascade of water.

Next we walked, huffing and puffing, through downtown
Brooklyn for about a mile, handing out antirecruitment and

propeace literature, singing "God Help America," our irrev-
erent antiwar version of the perennial patriotic staple. The
film crew interviewed several young people as we walked
along, and I was very impressed with their universal opposition to the war and their very articulate expression of their
views. One young woman impressed me so much with her
rhetoric that I practically begged her to run for office when
she completes college. Already, I was beginning to see that
we were going to learn as much as we hoped to teach on our
peacemaking quest.

We reached a recruiting center on Flatbush Avenue, where
Congressman Major Owens's son, Chris, greeted us with a
stirring speech and a very professional rendition of a gospel
song. Several Grannies went in to enlist but were politely
told to leave. We stood for a while outside the center and
sang songs, read our statement of purpose, and, finally, one
by one, placed a flower on the gate covering the doors of
the center as we sang "Where Have All the Flowers Gone?"

Ah, Staten Island, for us that day an island paradise. By
the time we arrived there, the rain had diminished to a slight
drizzle and the wonderful Staten Island Peace Action people,
led by Sally Jones, greeted us at Borough Hall with great
warmth and celebration. We stood on the steps of the hall
with our banners and bells as we read the names of the 118
New York State residents in the military who had perished
to date in Iraq, a sobering and profoundly moving task. One
of the Staten Island Peace Action members, Elaine Brower,
held a picture of her son currently stationed in Fallujah, adding
poignantly to the general sadness of the group. This is what
it's about for the Grannies—we don't want one more young
American military person to die or be maimed because our
cowardly president stubbornly refuses to carry out the people's will to end his misguided occupation of a country that
posed no threat.

After the activities had ended, a very exhausted, wet and bedraggled bunch of grandmas were then taken by our incredibly kind Staten Island hosts to slumber and revitalize for the heartwarming but difficult days ahead.

Day 2

The next day, Sunday, we went to Congressman Vito Fasella's offices, located in a mall. Vito has been a dedicated supporter of George Bush and has promoted the war in Iraq without pause ever since its inception. We spent a while there rallying outside on the street, urging drivers-by to reject the war, and were quite surprised at the number of drivers in conservative Staten Island who honked their horns in support of us.

But we had to move on. We were scheduled in Newark at noon, so we climbed back on the bus and departed New York's fifth borough. Now, we were leaving home ground and began to have a sense of actually being on a journey. It was a wistful and somewhat apprehensive feeling, at least for me.

Things did not go well in Newark. Arrangements got botched somehow and we weren't able to pull together a rally or event there. From Newark, I headed home for the night to write a column for Michael Moore's Web page while the Grannies continued on through North Plainfield and Trenton. I rejoined the group the next day in Philadelphia.

Days 3, 4, and 5: The Grannies (and Barbara Bush) Occupy Philadelphia

Day 3 was a jam-packed day in Philadelphia full of continual speaking, listening, and performing, beginning with an elegant breakfast forum at the White Dog Café near the University of Pennsylvania campus. This nonuniversity eatery is a really wonderful institution. In addition to providing good food and drink, it provides discussions and lectures on all manner of issues we Grannies are concerned with, runs community projects, promotes minority-run restaurants, serves as an art gallery and a concert venue, publishes cookbooks—well, the list of its activities and causes is infinite, practically. The entire operation is run by the incredible Judy Wicks.

At the White Dog, we had an opportunity to meet many local Philadelphia peace activists, to network and exchange ideas. Incidentally, if you've never visited Philadelphia, I urge you to do so. We Grannies found it stunningly beautiful as well as historically fascinating, and the university area is among the most lovely!

We followed the breakfast with a visit to the Stapley Senior Residence in another beautiful area, Germantown, full of gorgeous stone mansions and huge old trees. We spoke about the horrific costs of the war, performed our Granny Chorus Line song and dance, and I sang two of my original songs. Imagine our surprise when Barbara Bush came onstage and proceeded to speak to us and the Stapley residents about how devoted she and her son ("Georgie," she calls him) are to peace. She also explained to us that Georgie calls himself the Decider, an ironically inaccurate name when applied to him, we believe, in light of his reply when asked when he intends to bring the troops home: "It's up to the next president."

Mrs. Bush also assured us that we could all stop worrying about the high level of danger in Baghdad now that Saddam Hussein had been captured. She marveled at how safe Baghdad had become, as illustrated by the fact that Georgie was sneaked in and out of Baghdad in the dark of night back in June 2006 with an escort of only about ten armed helicopters and a few state-of-the-art military tanks. She told us that her boy was able to report that the Iraqi people are pleased we

> *"Sing your song of peace and hope. Yell imprecations at the warmongering profiteering killers of our children. Soothe a wounded soldier. Tell the children love will triumph and if we want to see the face of the deity, look into the face of the war orphan, and if we want to hear the voice of any God . . . just listen to the Grannies."*
> —Malachy McCourt

are there. As she said, "My son ought to know what the people think—after all, he spent the whole five hours he was in Baghdad talking only to the prime minister."

Confused? Don't be. As you've already probably guessed, this was the faux Barbara Bush, impersonated by our own Granny, Carol Husten.

At the end of our visit to the very impressive Stapley residence, we asked the members of the audience to tell us their names and make a brief statement. Many of them were in wheelchairs and were rather quiet during our presentation, causing us to wonder if they were indifferent to what we said, perhaps unconcerned and bored. To our pleased amazement, practically every one of them, mostly women, told us that they supported our antiwar stance completely.

Our final action on Tuesday was a meeting at the historic Friends Meeting House, where we listened to an Iraq War vet and an Iraqi woman describe the chaos and utter destruction created by our occupation. We also were privileged to hear the remarkable Sonia Sanchez recite her poetry.

Then it was our turn, and we pulled out all our performing stops, topped off by our own actress/playwright Vinie

Burrows, who recited a Langston Hughes poem that totally
wowed the audience. Next stop, Broadway. Oh, okay, Off-
Broadway!

On Wednesday, June 28, eleven grandmothers, residents
of the City of Brotherly Love, went to the main recruiting
center near City Hall. They went inside and asked to enlist,
and when denied permission to do so, refused to leave. Hours
passed by as they remained inside in a deadlock. We New
York grannies stood outside in a blazing sun chanting and
singing and showing in every possible way our support for
and love of the patriotic Philadelphians. Finally, near the end
of the day at the time the recruiting station was due to close,
the Philly Grannies were arrested and taken away to the police precinct. Among those arrested was Lillian Willoughby,
a 92-year-old wheelchair-bound local heroine famed for her
six-day incarceration two years earlier, when she blocked the
Federal Building in protest of our invasion of Iraq. Also arrested was the aforementioned poet, Sonia Sanchez.

By the time the Philadelphia Grannies were arrested, all
the local TV affiliates that had arrived to cover the story—
CBS, NBC, and ABC—had left to file their stories before
five P.M. So unfortunately, there was no footage showing the
Philadelphia women being taken away in the paddy wagon.
Savvy Bob Sann, our documentary producer, explained that
the military personnel in the recruiting station were well
aware that the media outside would have to turn in their stories for the evening broadcast and deliberately held the women
inside so it wouldn't be on the news.

It was a moving experience for us New York Granny jailbirds to witness others repeating our enlistment action and
realize that the movement of grandmothers in public resistance to the Bush administration's deadly, wrong-headed foreign policy was expanding.

By the end of our stay in Philadelphia, we were, to put it

succinctly, getting pooped. People in the upper ages don't react well to constant activity, sleeping in strange beds, eating meals on the run, and disrupted routines. But we had such exciting experiences and were so inspired by the brave grandmothers of Philadelphia that we were able to press on despite our growing discomforts and complaints. The next day, we weary wizened wanderers departed from Philly to meet Michael Berg and the peace community in Wilmington, Delaware.

Day 6: We Meet Michael Berg

The Granny Peace Brigade, that intrepid group of "Galloping Grannies" as one of our supporters tagged us, arrived in Wilmington, Delaware, on Thursday, June 29, where we had the honor of meeting with Michael Berg, the father of Nicholas Berg, the young entrepreneur executed in Iraq by beheading.

Michael Berg is a very thin, lively man of high intelligence and eloquently expressed opinions, a former high school teacher who at the time we met with him was running for Congress on the Green Party ticket. We met with him privately at an afternoon tea party he hosted at the Westminster Presbyterian Church, and later talked with him informally at the community church supper in our behalf.

At one point, I asked him if he could talk about his son or if he preferred not to. He said, "Oh, yes, I want to talk about him all the time; it keeps me going." He then described his son and vividly illustrated Nick's dedication to improving neglected areas of the world as he made repeated trips to African countries, where he helped install modern systems to benefit the residents.

Mr. Berg freely described his shock and grief upon learning of his son's awful death. We Grannies felt a deep sadness as we listened to him. How one could possibly cope with such a tragedy is really unimaginable, but he has put his terrible sorrow to productive use. He speaks powerfully and frequently of the need to end the occupation now and bring the troops home immediately. Our group felt enormous empathy for him and great admiration for his antiwar activism and tragedy-induced eloquence. As in all such heartrending situations, we were at a loss as to what to say to comfort him because we, of course, knew there *is* no comfort.

Wilmington may not be technically part of the South, but they gave us a sterling example of Southern hospitality nevertheless. We were fed three times in the half-day we were there, starting with a delicious lunch, followed by fruit and cookies offered by Mr. Berg during his afternoon tea forum, and, again, at the most savory potluck supper any of us had ever eaten. Yayyyy, Wilmington! I can still taste those curried vegetables, that sausage and sauerkraut combo, that pasta, that potato salad—and these are just maybe a tenth of what was served. The setting may have been less than elegant—a church basement—but the food was on a level of cordon bleu.

Once our bellies were full of food, we did our show, which included several songs, the Granny Chorus Line dance, and, the highlight of the evening, Vinie Burrows's recital of a great Langston Hughes poem. As usual, Vinie brought down the house.

I was particularly lucky to be assigned to a host family for the night in which the husband, Chuck Sutter, turned out to be a very hip jazz guitarist. We had a fine time listening to Bill Evans and other sundry bebop greats. I certainly lost some Manhattan elitism on my journey. Who says the only really hip people are in the Big Apple? We've met along the way the most sophisticated and aware people to be found anywhere.

Day 7

The next day, Friday, June 30, found us in a charming little town, Haddonfield, New Jersey, which, even though a mere dot on the map, had the biggest turnout yet for us, thanks to the exhaustive efforts of David Kalkstein, a leader in that town's Peace Action group. We spoke and performed in the town square and then held our vigil near their military recruitment center in front of a Starbucks. This is a juxtaposition that I can't account for, folks, unless it is loosely indicative of the relationship between the military and our industrial complex. Complex? More like an industrial psychosis, I'd say!

Later that day, we moved on to Princeton, where we marched in a parade led by a drum and fife trio of men dressed in Revolutionary military garb, which was a real trip! We arrived at a big open space in a lovely park where we were fed a picnic supper, after which we were presented with the annual Patriots Award by Rev. Bob Moore of Peace Action.

I was personally happy at the ceremony to see again Gold Star Mother Sue Niederer, whose son, Seth, was killed in Iraq in 2004. Sue has supported us in some of our actions and given amazing speeches about her son's death. Sue, a natural stand-up comedienne, does the impossible—talks of her terrible grief and yet during her presentations manages to be incredibly funny.

Days 9 and 10: Sweating It Out in the Nation's Capital

The Granny Peace Brigaders completed the final leg of their trek from New York City to Washington under a blazing sun in the nation's capital. But the extreme heat was not enough to curb our actions on July 3 and 4. Fortified with gallons of water, sun hats, and sunscreen, we elders walked and walked and stood for hours in the ninety-plus degree heat with no major physical mishaps.

Our Washington sojourn began on July 3 in Dupont Circle, where we were met by Cindy Sheehan, Daniel Ellsberg, Dick Gregory, Medea Benjamin, and others, all of whom escorted us on foot to the main event—a rally at the beautiful Gandhi Statue. Vinie Burrows gave one of her powerful extemporaneous speeches at both locations, which was widely quoted and televised in press and media all over the world. Other eloquent speeches were made by Ms. Sheehan, Mr. Ellsberg, Mr. Gregory, and a marvelous orator from San Francisco, Rev. Yearwood, who mesmerized the audience.

We encountered a disturbing counterprotest group—about a dozen people stood near us with a huge banner inscribed, "Cindy Sheehan's Starved for Attention," and other small degrading signs. It was extremely agitating to see these people berating a woman who had lost her son and has worked so tirelessly for peace. I had to contain myself from going over and giving them a good tongue-lashing. But what would have been the point? These people are cretins probably nurtured on a spiritual diet of Rev. Falwell and Joe McCarthy.

Our entire peace entourage then walked through northwest Washington to Lafayette Park across the street from the White House, where the Grannies chanted and sang and displayed their banners and signs right at the gate of the president's residence (at least on the rare occasions when he actually resides there). The same small group of counterprotesters with their nasty signs had followed us to the White House and stood near our antiwar group, babbling their mindless garbage, but we did our best to pay them no mind.

Speeches and songs by us and others in the crowd assembled in Lafayette Park filled the hot summer air, a perfect accompaniment to the many Code Pink people there preparing for a fast to begin at midnight. Two of our members—

Vinie Burrows and Diane Dreyfus—undertook the fast for
twenty-four hours in solidarity with the many people around
the world who stopped food intake in an act of protest against
the terrible war.

The next day, Independence Day! We knew we needed a
final attempt to awaken the public to the need for direct action to end the war in Iraq. Having had our fill of Bush's
residence the day before, we turned our attention to Dick
Cheney. Early in the morning, we hiked off to the Naval Ob-
servatory, the vice president's official residence, where we
again chanted and sang and generally vented our spleen at
this most horrendous of men. We were amazed at the number of drivers who honked in support of us as they drove
past. We were pleasantly surprised to see so much support
from such a tony neighborhood. Was this a sign of further
slippage of support for the Bushies, we fervently hoped?

After a long day of vigils and walks along the National Mall,
we piled wearily into our bus for the ride back to New York.
I was sitting near the front of the bus; when I looked toward
the rear, I saw approximately ten Grannies and Norman Siegel
sound asleep.

I griped a lot and felt tired a lot and certainly perspired a lot,
but, looking back, I am certain that we accomplished a lot—
encouraged people to exercise their Constitutional right to
dissent and demand an end to the occupation. I also had the
rare experience of seeing a large bunch of strong-minded,
opinionated older women closeted together for ten days survive arguments, clashes, even occasional angry words, and wind
up in the end still loving each other.

The consensus among the grannies about the trip was expressed well by one of our "baby grandmas," Ann Shirazi:
"The Granny trek demonstrated that a small group of ordinary people coming together with a common goal can make
the extraordinary happen. The unstinting support and gen-

erosity of groups committed to challenging this ruthless regime gave us the opportunity to touch the lives of those who have felt helpless and shut off because of this country's policies."

Also, our feelings were exemplified by Corinne Willinger, who possesses one of the four recent hip replacements among us: "Our trek was wonderful, exhausting, educational, profound, adventurous. I was able to experience an active, thoughtful, determined, powerful potpourri of women of various ages, opinions, and temperaments, but all with the same determination to get the message to the world that peace is not only possible but imperative."

Our documentary film producers, Bob Sann and Fran Sears, had a few words to say, also. They doggedly followed us the entire journey from beginning to end with their crew of ten, and so had an excellent overview. In their words, "The real gift of the Grannies is the living, breathing lesson they give every single day about what it is to be a participating member in our democracy. With these remarkable women on the road, we watched in awe as they tirelessly—and with humor and grace—kept spreading the word that 'Democracy is not a spectator sport.'"

Looking back, I believe our trek demonstrated the truth of the wise words of Dr. King:

Our lives begin to end the day we become silent about things that matter.

Chapter 9

Meeting Bill Clinton While Bird Dogging Hillary

> *I'm the very best candidate*
> *You couldn't ask for anything more*
> *So what if I triangulate*
> *When it comes to our kids at war?*
>
> —from the song "Hillary, Dillary Hawk"

Hillary Disappoints the Grannies

WE NEW YORK GRANNIES have always been puzzled by Hillary Clinton's popularity. As a matter of fact, we have singled her out for aggressive opposition. I personally began confronting her before the war began, when I went with a delegation of about ten people, at the behest of MoveOn, to plead with her to not sign the resolution giving George Bush the authority to launch a war on Iraq. We were not able to get an appointment with Ms. Clinton, but we were given permission to meet with some of her staff here in New York.

We spoke to several rather young aides. A very eloquent rabbi in our group argued the case against going to war, and I recall there was also among us a Middle East scholar as well as someone who had lived in Iraq for a few years, both of whom also spoke very convincingly of the folly of such an invasion. Ms. Clinton's staff was very receptive to what we were saying and, in fact, we had a definite sense that they agreed with us. All to no avail, unfortunately. As we all know, Hillary ignored the good advice we and others offered and voted for the resolution, an act which has reverberated negatively on her at times during her campaign for the presidency. She has shuttled back and forth from prowar to antiwar and back again—after she voted to give Bush authority to invade Iraq, she called for more troops to be sent there. Once she was well into her campaign, however, when there was much criticism of her wobbly stance, she started making noises about how she would end the war the day she assumed the presidency. But, then, another flip-flop—she refused to say whether she would end the war by 2013!

We Grandmothers have been very disappointed by her conflicting positions on the issue. After all, she represents New York City, the target of the 9/11 atrocity, and although we were the most afflicted by the terrorism, our city nevertheless has a strongly antiwar population. We could not comprehend how she could so misrepresent our wishes.

As she played politics with Bush's war, we began to get angry. Her votes for the Patriot Act—*twice*—really turned us off! We surmised early on that she seemed to have no core ethics to guide her, but based her decisions exclusively on her estimation of what would bring her the most votes when she ran for president. The last straw for us was when at the end of 2005 she cosponsored a bill to ban flag-burning, seemingly out of nowhere. It struck us as a pointless action, particularly in view of the fact there had been virtually no flag-burnings to speak of for many years. It was instead a strategic move to position herself favorably right smack in the political middle for a presidential run, and of absolutely no value in solving the really critical issues facing us. Well, the Grannies weren't going to stand for it!

We decided, along with members of Code Pink, that we would begin trailing her at her campaign events, where we would confront her on the issue of the war. The Grannies and the Code Pinkies picked a fund-raiser at the then trendy Manhattan club Crobar, for our first such bird-dogging event. We knew her husband, former president Bill Clinton, would be there shilling on her behalf, and he, as probably her chief strategist, seemed as good a target for us as Hillary.

Waiting for Bubba

Beverly Rice and I arranged to go inside to try and talk with Bill, while the rest of our group stood outside, wearing huge rubber ears, chanting, "Hillary, you're not listening."

Bev and I entered the popular new Manhattan club and walked around the plush, cavernous space. We were told people normally paid something like $500 just to get in to the Crobar, and spent another $150 merely to sit at a table. Luckily for us, we had a friend with an "in" and gained access for free. During the long wait for our friend to take us to the VIP room to meet Clinton, we discreetly laid a few pieces of our "army" (toy soldiers with the label "Bring me home") and a flier or two in the bathroom stalls. At last, we were ushered into the VIP room, a large bar, where a select group of people would be permitted to shake Bill Clinton's hand and be photographed with him. If we hadn't had an escort, it would have cost us $1,000 to enter that room. There was nothing to eat anywhere and the room was cold. A large crowd was waiting, like us, to see the popular ex-president. Most bought drinks from the bar to while away the time but I, practically a teetotaler, just stood and stood. The other people, we noticed, were almost all in their twenties and thirties.

Where *do* they get this kind of money, we wondered. This was a group I couldn't relate to—young, trendy, probably rich, probably club crawlers. Bev and I kept to ourselves. Finally, after what seemed an eternity, the big moment arrived. President Clinton walked into the room. He was tall, lean (he'd just had his heart bypass and had slimmed down considerably), and very, very attractive, highlighted by that mass of thick white hair. His smile illuminated the room like a hundred lights. We got into a single line and slowly inched our way up to him. I was trembling with nervousness. Beverly spoke to him first, introducing us. In a daze, I started babbling away while shaking his big, warm hand. I told him I was with the Grandmothers Against the War, and that we were the ones arrested at Times Square. I asked him if he knew about that, and he said yes. I wondered if he was telling the truth. I said that we hoped Hillary would get off the fence. He replied something to the effect of, "She's not sitting on the fence . . . there are several ways to view this," but didn't pursue it, and neither did I. I wasn't about to engage in a debate with a genius who has debated political issues all his life, as I knew he would make mincemeat of me, no matter how right I might be. I blurted out that I loved him. (Why did I say that? I liked some of his presidential decisions but deplored others, actually. It must have had something to do with the fact that I despised Bush so much at that point that Bill seemed like a god by comparison.) I said we didn't mean to be offensive but we wished his wife would call for an immediate end of

> *"You never really get to know anyone no matter how long you know them!"*
> —**Lillian Pollak**

the war. He assured me he was not offended. I told him we'd held a vigil at Rockefeller Center for two years and had devoted ourselves to ending the war. Then, like any awestruck teenage groupie, I gave him a piece of paper to sign, on which he wrote, "To Joan Wile. Thanks for your devotion to peace. Bill Clinton." I said "Thank you, President Kennedy." Realizing in acute agony what I'd just said, I told him, "Did you hear what I just called you—I said President Kennedy." He said, "That's all right." Our inside friend began making signals to us to wind up our encounter—we had already taken up much more time than the others. So, we left him, and he was on to the next person in line. Bev and I stumbled away in a state of shock.

We then went to the main ballroom, where we joined an enormous crowd gathered to hear his ten-minute speech. The guy is phenomenal—like a living computer. He spits out facts and figures as easily as the rest of us say "Good morning" and "Good night." It is rare to encounter a mind that digests and memorizes so much diverse information. While listening to his dazzling display of brains, one can't help but compare him with the present dunce occupying the White House. I felt extremely depressed at this thought.

Without mentioning the name of Bush, however, he shot quite a number of zingers at "the administration" as he discreetly referred to him—health care, tax cuts, the deficit, the disparity between rich and poor, and other topics. But, he did not refer to Iraq, just as Hillary had circumvented it in a recent campaign letter and questionnaire. Disappointing.

On the way home and during the rest of the night, I replayed my conversation with Bill Clinton a thousand times, only this time I said all the pungent, witty, and persuasive things I was too befuddled and overwhelmed to say when I spoke to him. My face got very tired from all the cringing I did as

I recalled my inadequate and horribly embarrassing performance.

Bev and I only hoped that our meeting may have been one more little nudge to get him to rethink Hill's position.

Another night in the annals of the Granny antiwar crusade.

The bird dogging of Hillary continues on to this day. There has been hardly a gala or party or rally for her that Code Pink anti-Hillary activists haven't been there with their chants and their signs. The very creative and bold (and young by comparison to us) Code Pink women have instigated some really fantastic actions towards Hillary; one of the more publicized ones was in Chicago, when she spoke to a huge crowd in an auditorium with balconies. At one point in her speech, they opened giant and very visible umbrellas from the balconies, emblazoned with messages exposing her support of the war. They also executed a very daring action at a fundraiser luncheon for the senator at the Hilton Hotel in Manhattan, at which the Senator thanked an endless list of supporters. And when she said "support" for the hundredth time, one of the Code Pinkies, Missy Beattie (who had recently lost her nephew in Iraq), stood up and shouted, "What about supporting our troops by bringing them home?" Two of the women removed the sweaters covering their pink T-shirts, on which they had written protroop messages with black fabric markers. (One said "2,475 U.S. military deaths: How many more?") Then they unfurled their pink satin "Troops home now" banners. As they started chanting, "Troops home now," the cameras strayed from Hillary toward the Code Pink ladies.

It would be so easy for Hillary to resolve her alienation from the peace movement if she'd just have the courage to admit that she should never have voted to allow Bush to carry out his evil plans against Iraq, that it was a bad mistake of her own judgment and that she can't blame it on the fact that she got wrong information from the Bush administration. If my Grannies and I, just ordinary citizens, could clearly see that we were being led with subterfuge and lies into a disastrous war, why couldn't she? We voted for her to *protect* our interests, not counter them. ⌇

— Chapter 10 —

Grannies Keep the Pressure On

I've got to take back my country
And I have no time to waste
Because we're facing catastrophe
The worst we've ever faced
    —from the song, "I've Got to Take Back My Country"

European Vigils

IN THE NEXT COUPLE OF MONTHS, we did a number of actions deserving of mention, while at the same time continuing with our weekly vigil at Rockefeller Center. It's worth noting that we have never, in the four years since the vigil began, missed a single one, even in terrible downpours. Among these diverse activities, a second group of Grannies went to Germany, this time visiting not only Berlin but other towns and cities.

Many people don't know it, but Germany is the main European base for extreme rendition and transport of U.S. military personnel and equipment to and from Iraq and Afghanistan, as well as containing the biggest U.S. air field on foreign soil, the biggest military hospital, and the largest military community abroad. Germany's former chancellor, Gerhard Schröder, had been staunch in attempting to stop the war before it began, along with France's president, Jacques Chirac. Shamefully, our government chastised the two countries for their stance (you'll recall the dreaded "freedom fry" in lieu of "french fry"). However, we Grannies were very grateful for the backbone the two countries demonstrated when they refused to support the United Nations amendment approving the invasion of Iraq. In fact, I even e-mailed letters of support to the French and German ambassadors to the UN. A fat lot of good their opposition did, I'm sorry to say.

A huge protest was planned on July 13, 2006—the day of Bush's arrival in Chancellor Merkel's home town, Stralsund. Elsa Rassbach, an American living in Berlin for many years and a member of an antiwar coalition American Voices Abroad, thought it would be significant for Europe's peace movement if American antiwar grandmothers would join them for the anti-Bush rally. Our Grannies did not hesitate.

On July 11, 2006, four of our members—Barbara Walker, Betty Brassell, Susan Nickerson, Ann Shirazi, and her husband, Ahmad, as well as one non-Granny, Laurie Arbeiter, flew to Germany. They were joined by a sixth member of the Granny Peace Brigade, Diane Dreyfus, who had been visiting in Amsterdam.

When our representatives arrived in Stralsund the day before Bush's scheduled appearance, a large, friendly crowd greeted them.

We grannies had all recently started wearing black T-shirts bearing the slogan, "We will not be silent." They were designed and manufactured by Laurie, a young artist (young as compared to us, anyway—in her forties), who conceived the idea when she learned of the White Rose Society, which was the name of a group of five German students and their philosophy professor at the University of Munich who made and distributed leaflets in 1942 and 1943, calling for people to rise up against Hitler and the war. Their slogan was, "We will not be silent." Tragically, they were all executed by the Nazis, but their story of extreme courage and commitment lives on to inspire others to oppose tyranny.

The Grannies wore their T-shirts at the gathering, and Laurie accompanied them with two big boxes of the shirts in different sizes to sell (or give, in many cases) to the German group. The next day, at the demonstration for Bush's arrival, the women were surprised and certainly pleased to see that practically everybody in the crowd was wearing them.

The Grannies got wide coverage in the German press and media and, at the end of the trip, felt a tremendous sense of accomplishment. As Barbara Walker commented, "That week was one of my most moving, stirring, stunning experiences (and I have been having experiences for seventy-three years)."

But Germany was not the only European nation on our agenda. Dr. Pat Salomon, our only non-New York member, happened to be visiting London for a wedding, when the Grannies received an invitation to speak at a very important international peace conference there. Pat somehow sneaked a speech to the meeting in between wedding activities.

It felt good to know that our group was represented in two European countries and that these populations, which were and are so heavily opposed to America's foreign policies, were exposed through us to an awareness of the strong and growing opposition to the Iraq disaster among the American public. Ann Shirazi visited her husband's family in Tehran and spread the word there that many Americans are absolutely opposed to bombing that country. Additionally, Vinie Burrows, Carol Husten, and Phyllis Cunningham attended a Women's International Democratic Federation conference in Venezuela in April 2007, the theme of which was "Women in Strug-

> *"Keep going, hating war, injustice, protesting, loving life."*
> —Lillian Pollak

gle." Perhaps we should call ourselves the Jet-Set Grandmas. Undoubtedly by the time this manuscript is published, the Grannies will have traveled further around the world!

On Home Ground

Back on our home turf, New York City, the Grannies made more and more appearances—on radio, television, and at meetings, classes, seminars, and campaign fund-raisers, sometimes speaking and sometimes doing our act. I personally sang on WBAI radio, on Air America, and on a public access television program, *The Ronnie Eldridge Show*. Ronnie is a former New York City councilwoman, and a terrific one at that, who had to give up the position as a result of New York's two-terms limit law. We certainly miss her. She is also married to the famous columnist and author Jimmy Breslin, which I suspect is a full-time job in itself. For one thing, the guy doesn't drive, so Ronnie has to lug him all over the place to investigate and interview people for his far-flung stories. Inasmuch as the person she serves, though, is a great writer and truth-teller, it's undoubtedly a worthy endeavor.

Another time, Carol Husten and I schlepped way out in Queens to make a presentation to a class at York College, a part of the City University system. Two professors led the class—Michael Flynn, a psychologist, and Vadim Moldovan, a Russian-born assistant professor of social work. Their objective in holding the class was to try to stimulate activism in what appears to be a largely apathetic student population, seemingly all over America. But, this did not strike us as the case among the students we spoke to. They were young and informed, and some were actively involved in protesting the war.

We explained the purpose of Grandmothers Against the War in hopes of motivating them to organize as we did. I also threw in what I call my "call-to-arms" song, "Grannies, Let's Unite," which they seemed to enjoy. It was gratifying to me, because although it always got a rousing response from older people, I was afraid it wouldn't have much appeal for young adults. The young people asked intelligent and penetrating questions and expressed impassioned opposition to the war. We were extremely impressed with the commitment of the two professors to making their students aware of the terrible quagmire our government had pushed us into. Without a draft to scare our youth into mobilizing against the war, as the nation's young people did during the Vietnam War, it seems to me our best recourse for awakening them is their teachers. And, as is so often the case, we wound up being more stimulated and hopeful as a result of our pep talk than were even the people we were supposed to be firing up.

On another occasion, we had the pleasure of traveling to Brooklyn to receive an award from the Ethical Culture Society, which is housed in an exquisite mansion on a lovely tree-lined street—I don't think the rest of the world is aware of how beautiful many parts of Brooklyn are. And, also, of course, how varied.

Throughout it all, my trio of professional singers, the New York Granny Chicks, continued to perform—at campaign events, peace rallies, fund-raisers, and the like. It was fun for us three old dames, all in our seventies, to sing in public again after our performing lives had diminished considerably, and especially to do so in the cause of peace. I felt a terrible loss when Helen Miles, one of the trio and a marvelous woman, died suddenly in the summer of 2007.

The Granny Peace Brigade also headed a huge peace march in the summer of 2006. It was a long walk, but we made it—three-plus miles from near the United Nations all the way down Broadway to Foley Square in lower Manhattan. Also, it was blazingly sunny, a challenge we met triumphantly. We pushed in wheelchairs four Grannies who couldn't walk for long stretches, which, I admit somewhat sheepishly, made for a very good visual for the many cameras who snapped our pictures as we walked by.

Everything we did as a group and individually certainly contributed to our growth and evolution as significant players in the urgent quest to end the occupation of Iraq. Many activities and encounters, many learning experiences, and much gratifying recognition—but so many hopes unrealized for a cessation of the war. ⌒

— Chapter 11 —

Growing Pains

Get me out of here
I've really got to go
I can't stand this atmosphere
I'd rather be in Guan-tan-a-mo!!
—from the song "The Inner Laura Bush"

The Elephant in the Room

I HAD HEARD FROM PEOPLE who had spent more time than I had working within volunteer organizations that there often came a moment when the differences of opinion between people collided so explosively that groups broke apart, or almost did. I thought that our Grannies were united as if we were glued together, and I was fully confident our solidity could not be broken. I was in for an unpleasant surprise.

It happened in July 2006 during a regular monthly meeting at which we were discussing, as usual, our next moves in our efforts to end the occupation of Iraq. Suddenly, Carol Husten said, "We're sitting here talking as if nothing has happened when there's this elephant in the room." She was referring to the clash between Israel and Lebanon, and the recent bombings by Israel ostensibly in retaliation for Hezbollah attacks and kidnapping of Jewish soldiers. She and others in the group wanted the Granny Peace Brigade to denounce Israel publicly. Immediately, a huge chasm opened up that threatened to swallow us all. A lot of suppressed emotion and anger erupted to the surface.

A number of the women, quite a few of them Jewish, were angry with Israel for its actions. One or two supported Israel, but with great trepidation about stating their position for fear of being ostracized for what they felt the majority of the group considered a politically incorrect stance. Others, me among them, felt the issue was far too explosive and historically tangled for us to make a knowledgeable and objective judgment and did not want our group to take a stand at all. One person referred to "the Zionist lobby," which served only to inflame the situation further. Despite the intense wishes of the anti-Israel group that we support Lebanon, it was finally decided that a special meeting would be held shortly for the sole purpose of attempting to resolve our conflict.

The turmoil of the evening left many of us quite upset. I felt that I couldn't continue being part of a group that was so contrary to my political thinking, a feeling later I learned was shared by some of the others. I had founded Grandmothers Against the War and then later helped initiate the Granny Peace Brigade for the sole purpose of trying to bring the troops home from Iraq. I felt everything I had been working toward crumbling apart in this ideological friction. If we were to become mired in this dispute, I feared we would lose our focus on the issue that had brought us together and mobilized us in the first place.

We scheduled a special meeting later to try to resolve our conflict. I had secretly determined that I would not attend the special meeting and would phase out of the Granny group. But fate works in mysterious ways. As it turned out, the designated meeting place for the special meeting was unavailable and the only place it could be held wound up being my living room. I couldn't very well escape that!

Dr. Pat Salomon, who was in New York for the meeting, said she had a plan for resolving our conflict. She put up a huge easel with blank pages on which were to be written all the things we could agree on. One by one, we offered up our thoughts:

"We want strife in the Middle East to end."

"We want no preemptive wars."

"We don't want our country to conduct bombings which hurt civilians."

If someone suggested a policy or a wish that all couldn't endorse, it did not get written down. Soon there was quite a long list—so long, in fact, that we were able to realize that we still had a lot in common, in terms of our social and political beliefs.

Despite our ability to agree on certain points, the issue of Lebanon and Israel kept rearing its ugly head and arguments would begin all over again. It was very hot, the Grannies were getting tired after several hours of engaging in such an

"Everyone's experiences are different, influenced by their past, their families, their class, their culture, whether they've experienced hardship, been discriminated against or mistreated, isolated or surrounded by humanity. Try not to judge or prejudge. Take positions on what you know is right and what is wrong, and fight for your beliefs."
—Corrine Willinger

intense exercise, and tempers flared. Although we had made a mighty effort and come to some sort of rapprochement, the hostilities still lurked under the surface. We were definitely not in the same accordance as we had been before the Israel-Lebanon impasse had developed.

By the end of the meeting, we had appointed a committee of five Grannies to meet privately at a later date to draw up a mission statement that we could *all* live with—one that encompassed our areas of solidarity and avoided the ones of discord. We would vote on it at the next meeting, in an effort to calm the storm.

With great anxiety, I awaited the next meeting and the reading of the statement the subgroup had written:

> We, the Granny Peace Brigade, stand for peace. We oppose the use of military force to resolve conflicts between nations or hostile forces.
>
> In case of war we advocate:
>
> Immediate and unconditional cease-fire.
>
> Meeting of all hostile forces directly involved, with a neutral independent mediator to resolve the conflict and establish a permanent peace.
>
> No United States engagement in preemptive war actions.

There was nothing in that statement that any of us couldn't subscribe to no matter what our position on the Israel-Lebanon muddle was. We all breathed a big sigh of relief and we moved on to the next subject on our agenda—Grandparents Day plans, if I remember correctly. For the moment, we had a tentative solution.

Despite our differences, we found a way to go on as a group. Perhaps Pat's crisis resolution plan alleviated some of the tensions. Perhaps the fact that Israel and Lebanon reached a détente of sorts on their own helped. Whatever the reason, the Granny Peace Brigade stayed together without losing a single member. "Thank heavens," is all I can say. Because, as it turned out, there were many accomplishments and adventures awaiting us still. ⌒⌒

— Chapter 12 —

Not Your Usual Grandparents Day

In the time that's left to me
I'll continue to strive
To take back my country
As long as I'm alive

> —from the song "I've Got to Take Back
> My Country"

Balloons and Boos

IN THE SUMMER OF 2006, we had surmounted our crisis and were still together. The time had come to do something extraordinary again. We felt a desperate compulsion to put together an event that would get the attention of the sluggish public, which, although increasingly negative about the war in Iraq, nevertheless was torpid about aggressively opposing it. I don't believe it was just the heat of summer that was responsible for this lethargy, either. Not being a political analyst or a sociologist, I can only give a very uneducated guess as to why Americans seemed completely indifferent to this horrible war, except for a small percentage, like us Grannies, who literally felt it in our bones to the exclusion of all other matters.

I believe the lack of a draft has something to do with it. We can be fairly certain that if a draft were to be initiated, college campuses would explode with outrage and the war would be quickly concluded. But the public's inertia might also be partially a result of Americans being unable to confront the fact that we could possibly be in the wrong about our invasion of Iraq. The attack on the World Trade Center had cast us as innocent victims of evil terrorists, and we thought of ourselves, consequently, as the good guys. But Iraq had absolutely nothing to do with that catastrophe, and our invasion of that country was ethically reprehensible and entered into under false pretenses. It was morally indefensible. For a long time, America couldn't face up to the injustice of our invasion of a sovereign nation that had meant us no harm.

I also attribute the passiveness of the American people to what appears to be a basic lack of empathy or, perhaps, imagination, in the American sensibility. There's a sort of arrogance involved that sometimes prevents Americans from feeling the pain of those from other cultures to the extent we feel our own. An Iraqi child wounded by our bombs doesn't grab our hearts the same way that a hurt American child does. An African toddler visibly starving doesn't arouse our sympathy as much as a hungry American baby. Something like that, maybe, explains the American indifference to the terrible suffering caused by our invasion and occupation of Iraq.

And, let us not forget, there has been a news blackout since the beginning of the occupation of Iraq so that we almost never see the coffins of dead American military personnel or horribly wounded survivors. Thus, our citizens have been largely unaware of the heavy price paid by our armed forces, and this also accounts for the tragic lack of concern for the human costs of the war.

By the time September 2006 arrived, a general awareness had grown across the nation that we couldn't justify this war, that it was not defensible morally, and that the only responsible thing to do was to get out. Unfortunately, even with this shift in the public attitude, we were practically helpless to effect an end to the conflict as long as our seemingly intractable, hopelessly blind president stubbornly refused to enact the people's will; and I fear that by the time of publication of this book, we will *still* be trapped in the quagmire of Iraq. My God, I hope I'm wrong!

Despite the feeling that we were fighting against all odds, however, we pressed on. We decided that an opportune time to conduct a new action would be on Grandparents Day, September 10. We tossed around various ideas for a while, none of which seemed to jump out as either unusual or spectacular enough to attract attention from what we had depressingly learned was the absolutely necessary press and media. Too bad, isn't it, that we have to sell urgently needed causes the same way we push paper towels and deodorants, or any of the other items commonplace in TV commercials these days, most of which would have made my grandmother faint if she were alive to see them. Betty Coqui, remembering our walk across the Brooklyn Bridge at the beginning of our trek to Washington, suggested we cross that bridge again, this time reversing the direction and coming to Manhattan from Brooklyn. We liked her idea, hoping that on this occasion we'd have sunshine rather than the torrential rain we endured the first time.

We decided to make our walk as much like a parade as possible, complete with beating drums. We arranged to carry twenty-five enormous black balloons, three feet in circumference, emblazoned with the words, "Troops home now." The cost was $600, including delivery, very necessary considering the size of the merchandise—we couldn't even fit *one* in a taxi! This was quite expensive for a bunch of grandmothers mostly on modest fixed incomes, but we felt it was so important to draw new attention to our cause. As it turned out, the expenditure was well worth it.

We put the word out, and September 10, 2006, dawned sunny and warm. Approximately two hundred people assembled in a park in Brooklyn near the bridge. Even as I approached our meeting place, I saw the balloons—immense and incredibly eye catching. I was proud to participate in our parade that day, even though I couldn't walk. I had to be pushed in a wheelchair because I had just suffered an attack of gout and was not ambulatory. It is really embarrassing to admit to having had gout—most people immediately associate it with obese old drunken kings who ate entire suckling pigs at never-ending orgiastic feasts. But I am neither male, nor, I hasten to add, a drinker, and certainly most definitely not royalty.

A wonderfully kind male stranger, Mel, a nurse by profession, pushed me across the bridge. We were accompanied by a colorfully dressed Buddhist monk banging a cymbal, by drummers, antiwar activists of all stripes, grandpas and our ubiquitous Grannies, all wearing our signature "We will not be silent" T-shirts and carrying, of course, our huge, impossible-to-ignore balloons. We also carried a life-size cardboard coffin covered with an American flag, to bring home the point that this fun parade had the serious purpose of reminding people that our troops were dying every day.

When we reached the Manhattan side of the bridge, right next to City Hall, we held a press conference for the many photographers and reporters waiting there. We had as speakers a coterie of faithful local politicians, who we can almost always count on to show up; the president of the local chapter of Veterans for Peace; our "star" Granny and incomparable speaker, actress Vinie Burrows; and an Iraq vet who was part of a relatively new group, Iraq Veterans Against the War. He was particularly effective in his description of the hor-

> *"If not me, who? If not now, when?"*
> —**Marlena Santoyo**

rors of the conflict in Iraq and his belief, along with others in his group, that the war was a waste and a crime. It's hard to argue with someone who has been there and sacrificed so much.

Next on the agenda was a walk to Ground Zero. Again, the angelic Mel pushed my wheelchair, as we marched through the streets of downtown Manhattan to the site of the World Trade Center atrocity. I had seen it several times before, but always the immensity of the hole in the ground is a big shock, and standing there one has to try to push away unbearable images of people jumping to their deaths from those towering heights or being crushed beneath unthinkable tons of debris. We positioned ourselves right in front of the pit with our banners and our coffin, and held our balloons aloft. We knew George Bush was scheduled to arrive at Ground Zero that afternoon, and he couldn't fail to see our giant balloons, we figured, unless he covered his eyes, which he might well have wanted to do. After all, he had been warned of a possible attack on that site a month before it happened and if the man had a shred of guilt (unlikely) he would have wanted to avoid being reminded of his catastrophic mistake.

We waited for several hours in the hot sun for the president to make his obligatory token visit, but not without some excitement. Laurie Arbeiter, the T-shirt artist, managed to get herself arrested when a policeman ordered her to move from where she stood, just a few feet from the Grannies.

"You need a permit to stand there," he barked.

"I have a permit," Laurie responded, and showed him a copy of the Constitution she carries.

At that point, he brutally hustled all one hundred pounds of her to a patrol car and drove her to a precinct. People shouted, "Shame, Shame," and several Grannies jumped into a taxi and followed her there, where she was held for a long time. "You hurt me," she told the arresting officer when she was released. "I know," replied this marvelous specimen of New York's Finest.

Finally, George and Laura Bush arrived at Ground Zero. There were no sirens, just a lot of black cars before and aft his big black limousine. "What a farce," I thought, "Bush pretending to mourn the dead of 9/11 while forcing our military personnel to die in Iraq daily." (I feel fairly confident many others saw the irony of it, too.) Jenny Heinz shouted at his limo, "Impeach Bush! You are the war criminal!" Did he see us or hear Jenny's scream? I hope so, but because his car had one-way windows, we couldn't see through from the outside, we couldn't observe his expression. But it would have been difficult for him to miss the balloons.

At least, the press noticed them. There were many pictures on the evening news and in the next day's newspapers of the crowds crossing Brooklyn Bridge and those at Ground Zero—dominated impressively by our twenty-five black balloons soaring overhead with the words clearly stating, "Troops out now." Well, maybe just twenty-four. I believe one burst somewhere along the way.

But, Grandparents Day wasn't entirely over, at least not for Molly Klopot, Barbara Walker, and me. We went to a fancy restaurant across the street from Lincoln Center, where we received an award from the Park River Independent Democrats (PRID) for our efforts on behalf of peace. Also receiving an award that night from PRID was one of the greatest journalists in America, past or present, who in a time of media corruption unparalleled in our history always speaks the truth—Jimmy Breslin. What a thrill to share such an honor with him.

The food was pretty good, too!

It would have been nice to spend Grandparents Day with my grandchildren, I suppose—observing them in my usual disgustingly adoring fashion, possibly playing Monopoly with them, maybe even being given a handmade card or two, and, best of all, some hugs. But, perhaps this had been a better way to celebrate the occasion, after all—trying as best as I knew how to protect their futures so they could live in peace and not be used as cannon fodder someday in a war to satisfy the greed of a few men. ⌒

— Chapter 13 —

Let's Get On with the Show!

Don't put me out to pasture
Let me play my part
Time goes by so fast, you're
There before you start
—from the song "I'll Keep on Keeping On"

Performance for Peace

IT WAS REALLY DIFFICULT, at times, to keep up our momentum, to dream up and implement intriguing actions that would maintain public awareness. Without that recognition, of course, we couldn't hope to affect any change in the direction of our country regarding the war. What could we come up with next?

In the winter of 2006, we decided to put on a show (does this remind you of those old Mickey Rooney/Judy Garland musicals?). We had been adding on to it bit by bit. As previously described, I had first written and performed my original songs either solo or with my trio, the New York Granny Chicks. We Grannies then created our chorus line to our song, "There's No Business Like War Business." Next, I wrote a comedy monologue for Carol Husten, a very funny lady, to do as Barbara Bush. Vinie Burrows did her powerful dramatic monologues and poetry recitations (often by Langston Hughes).

For some reason, I decided it would be good if we added a short one-act play, too. Partly, I wanted to give some of the other Grannies a chance to strut their stuff, and partly—well, I don't know really why—it just struck me as a good idea.

I had never written a play before, although I had written songs for a number of musicals, and often wrote the dialogue as well. So, I wasn't entirely inexperienced, but still I felt a bit daunted at the prospect. Nevertheless, and don't ask me how, fairly soon we had a one-act play ready for performance, entitled *Molly Gets a Life*.

I cast Nydia Leaf, Barbara Walker, Ann Shirazi, and Jenny Heinz in the main parts. The only thing we needed was a director. I certainly didn't feel qualified for that job. My talents are limited to writing and singing, and I knew I was lousy at managing people as one would have to do skillfully as a director. At first, I considered asking Vinie Burrows to direct the one-act, but I was embarrassed to. Her experience was so vast in the theater as an actress, director, and playwright that I felt my little project was really beneath her. And, besides, I couldn't evaluate whether it was any good. I couldn't ask a professional like Vinie to work with what might be a very inferior product.

Then, instinct pointed me to Fran Sears . . . thank heavens. Fran and her husband, Bob Sann, had been part of our little band of agents provocateurs since the early summer of 2006, when they decided to make a documentary of our ten-day trek to Washington. Since the trip, they were honorary members of the brigade, attending our meetings, participating in our actions, and on many occasions advising us. I knew that Fran had a long career as a producer, particularly in television—after-school specials, soap operas, and the like, and did some directing, too. Impressed with Fran's intelligence and aura of capability, I asked her if she would take on this rather frightening project—directing a bunch of old biddies with no experience, in a short play written by another old biddy! I felt the same trepidation as I had about Vinie in asking Fran, a seasoned professional, to work with what might be—well, there's no other way to define it, folks, sorry—a piece of crap. But, Fran, considerably younger than me, was not quite as intimidating as Vinie. I screwed up my courage, I asked her, and she said yes.

With the addition of my new material to our presentation, I suddenly realized, "My God, we will have a full-fledged cabaret show ready to be produced." Naturally, it became crucial that we have a chance to put it all together and show it to the public somewhere. That's when our dear friend, Vietnam vet Hugh Bruce, came into the picture.

You'll recall that Hugh was the Vet for Peace who "escorted" a nasty heckler by the scruff of the neck down the street to the cops in one of our early vigils. Since then, he had been one of our most loyal supports. He rarely failed to attend our vigils on Fifth Avenue, came to our demonstrations, and, now, suddenly emerged as our "angel" in putting on our show.

Hugh is one of the most surprising people I've ever known. A Brooklyn man of Irish descent, his outward personna is not tough, exactly, but maybe one could say "crusty" at times. He's someone you wouldn't want to mess with, in other words. At the time he began joining the vigil, he was vice president

> *"You have a first amendment right to peacefully protest. Use it. Otherwise, that right will atrophy."*
> —**Norman Siegel**

of the New York Chapter of Veterans for Peace, having served in Vietnam as a medic on the front lines. He later became a chaplain, which fact also seemed somewhat incongruous to the outward person the world sees. Hugh is also openly gay, and never has hidden it, even when its revelation could have caused him harm. When he returned from Vietnam he joined two organizations, Viet Vets Against the War, and the Mattachine Society (the first group to advocate for human rights for gays in the United States). Two years later, the Stonewall Riot occurred and the rest is history. We Grannies admire him tremendously for the courage he has shown in straightforwardly being himself, no matter what the cost. It is my hope that this description of a terrific guy might alleviate, to some extent, any prejudice on the part of my readers toward gay men and women.

Hugh is very closely allied with St. Luke in the Fields church in Greenwich Village—as an usher, a coconvenor of its Peace and Justice Committee, and a cofounder of the church's Saturday Dinner for Persons with AIDS, now in its nineteenth year of operation. The church is housed in an exquisitely beautiful structure and provides much artistic and social sustenance to its community. As Hugh, himself, says: "I love the St. Luke's community and their brave and constant efforts on behalf of the sick, the poor, and disenfranchised. Needless to say, they are a 'peace church.' "

Hugh suggested that perhaps we might do a performance of my "playlet," as I called it, at his church. He immediately went about arranging for us to do *The Granny Peace Brigade Cabaret* on Sunday, December 3, 2006.

With only about two weeks to prepare, I went into a flurry of writing new songs, creating new material for "Barbara Bush," and working on play revisions. The cast began chaotically rehearsing, as well, causing everybody to feel frantic and discombobulated. I don't think there was more than one

actual complete rehearsal with the full cast until the dress rehearsal in the church, which was a shambles so extreme that
I can't bear to think about it much less relate it here. Poor
Fran was understandably a nervous wreck—trying to coordinate amateur actors with hardly any rehearsal under their
belts, complicated sets with no furniture or props, no space
to perform but just a corner of the cafeteria with a few boards
for a stage, and no lighting except the on-off lights. You get
the idea.

Sunday morning dawned. The telephone rang early. I sensed
bad news, and I was right. Helen Miles, one of the New York
Granny Chicks scheduled to sing solo my new song, "The
Inner Laura Bush," was unable to perform. I couldn't sing it
and play the piano accompaniment at the same time—it required a stand-up performance, so I had to drop the number. What else could go wrong?

We got to the church and discovered that the room we
were slated to perform in, the aforementioned cafeteria, was
completely occupied by about two hundred people as part of
a regular after-service coffee hour. Obviously, they had no knowledge that there was to be a performance but instead milled
around talking loudly to one another with little apparent interest in seeing our show. There was no place for us to perform and no chairs were arranged for an audience, if there
was to be one, to observe us. The platforms we had laboriously helped carry the day before up about fifty flights (it
seemed) from the bowels of the church, and which we were
to utilize as our stage, had vanished. On and on, the cata-
strophes piled up until Fran, at one point, shrieked, "Let's
forget it . . . there's no way we can do this." Disconsolate, we
prepared to abandon ship.

But, in the old tradition of "the show must go on," at the
last-minute things began to miraculously fall in place and
we were able to perform after all. We noticed that chairs

were suddenly produced, a set was hastily rigged with a kind of curtain for actors to make entrances and exits, and an audience of about one hundred people began taking their seats. In a frenzy, we hastily donned our costumes in an adjacent gym—and, by that special magic that seems to attend even the most primitive production, we got on with the show.

Judging from audience reaction, I'd say that our performance went over very well. Even the playlet fared all right. I heard some laughs, although I was in such a state of nervous anxiety, not only about the untested worth of the play but about the chaotic circumstances we'd had to deal with, that I probably couldn't gauge audience reaction very accurately. But, it was a triumph, of sorts, and new stars were born—our two leads, Nydia Leaf and Barbara Walker. Yes, they were in their seventies, to be sure, but nevertheless on December 3, 2006, the two emerged as theatrical divas. Another star materialized, too, one in her late eighties—Molly Klopot. Molly didn't want to be the "sexy" entr'acte sign carrier called for in the script. She resisted and resisted. But, when at the last minute we prevailed upon her to go out and do it, she slinked and slanked across the stage with such saucy abandon that she brought the house down each of the three times she sashayed across the floor. Perhaps she wouldn't admit it, but I am positive Molly had the time of her life. ⌒⌒

— Chapter 14 —

3,000 GI Deaths

The kids are dying
far away in foreign lands
I must keep on trying
their lives are in my hands
    —from the song "I've Got to Take Back My Country"

A Day of Mourning

CHRISTMAS 2006 WAS COMING, but the troops still weren't coming home. The war was edging toward its fifth year, longer than World War II. Those of us committed to ending the occupation wondered how people could fully celebrate the holidays, knowing that so many of our American kids were dying and being grievously wounded and Iraqis were suffering daily horrors of destruction and deprivation. We had hopes, however, that the Democrats, who were now to be in the majority in the House and Senate as a result of the election in November, would turn things around once they were sworn in. All we could do in the meantime was to "keep on keeping on," as Marie Runyon often said. We continued to write and call our new representatives to urge them to do all within their power to stop the slaughter.

As the New Year approached, it became apparent that we would soon reach the unthinkable—the three thousandth GI death count in Iraq. We knew we would have to publicly acknowledge this tragic milestone in a manner that would have a strong impact on people, help make them alarmed enough about the disastrous consequences of the war to stand up and oppose it. I received an impassioned e-mail from Cindy Sheehan's sister, Dede, urging that we figure out a way together to implement such a reminder and pay tribute to those brave souls who'd lost their lives for questionable motives of the president and his administration.

It was difficult to plan for this event because, of course, we didn't know precisely what day would be the one when the awful announcement would be made. I felt rather ghoulish about it, but I did some mental calculations based on the recent pattern of casualties and estimated that it would fall within the next two to three weeks. Then I did an e-mail blast, telling people that we would hold a vigil at our regular site in front of Rockefeller Center on the day after the three-thousand-GI death toll was officially reported. Unhappily, that news came on New Year's Day. With sadness, I sent out an announcement to my list announcing that our Day of Mourning 3,000 would be held on the next day, Monday, January 2, 2007.

What a painful way to begin a new year—acknowledging the deaths of so many mostly young people on the brink of life with goals, hopes, and plans for what they hoped would be long lives ahead. And, what made it even worse, from the Grannies' perspective, was that their lives were tossed away so carelessly by a man blinded and twisted by greed, a mountain-size but totally baseless ego, distorted ambition, and heartlessness. I know, his whole administration played key roles, but as George W. Bush himself said, "I'm the decider," so he must take the ultimate responsibility. I, for one, will never, never forgive him for bringing so much harm to our country and the entire world.

> *"Listen to your granny!"*
> —Marjorie Lasky

On the day after the New Year officially began, somewhere around one hundred people gathered on our Fifth Avenue spot in the late afternoon. I was astonished at the numbers—until that day, the largest group that had ever assembled was on the day Cindy Sheehan joined us, when approximately sixty people showed up. On this day of mourning, we took up the entire block between 49th and 50th Streets. We had obtained a list of names of the dead, and a small group began to read them at one end of the line. Ann Shirazi brought her meditation bell, which she would gently strike once after each name was read. Among the readers was our dear friend and defender, Norman Siegel, and another dear friend, Malachy McCourt.

Many of you are familiar with Malachy. He is, to be sure, the brother of the Pulitzer Prize–winning author, Frank McCourt (*Angela's Ashes*), but more, much more, than that is the fame he has earned by virtue of his own career—as an actor; the author of the books *A Monk Swimming*, *Bush Lies in State*, and others; a candidate for governor of New York in 2006; a radio show host; a columnist—and certainly for his larger-than-life persona. Malachy is a big, hearty Irishman with a brogue almost as thick as his girth. He has a huge heart and an enormous wit, and has always boldly fought visibly and audibly for progressive causes. This giant of a man (in every sense) has been very supportive of the Grannies— he has written beautiful and poetic messages to us that have been very inspiring when we embarked on some of our more challenging actions, and has been there when we needed him. Here is one of my favorite letters sent to us at the start of our trek to Washington the summer of 2006:

> *My dear rebel for peace Joan:*
>
> *As I will not be in NYC at the start of your great quest for peace and justice—I want you and your fellow questors to know that I'll be with you in spirit every step of the way. If there is a God then she will surely shower your pilgrimage with a surplus of blessings and hosannas in the highest. America has tried the man way of doing the nation's business and it has failed abysmally. Now is the time to do it the Grannies way all the way and to try in court all the men responsible for the slaughter and rapine in Iraq and elsewhere.*
>
> *To you, Joan, and all the pilgrims for peace with you, may the sun shine gently on your graying heads—may your shoes have wings to lift you when the going gets tough—may your hearts be filled with love all the way and may all the birds and all the people of this glorious land raise their voices in a paean of praise for your courage and sacrifice and a prayer for the restoration of these United States and the Constitution to the people where they belong. Come triumphant bearing the cup of democracy overflowing with freedom, liberty and peace.*
>
> *Thank you from Malachy McCourt*

As we began the task of mourning the three thousandth GI death on this cold January day, two less welcome people stood just feet away from our vigil. They were two counter-protesters with a group called United American Committee. They held U.S. flags and their own signs, with such messages as, "We shall stay the course. Keep the promise. No surrender" and "Warning: Leftist protesters trying to demoralize our troops." Their leader, Pamela Hall, said that our group's messages were "antipatriotic and disrespectful." This is reflective of the chasm in our society created by the conflict in Iraq. Those of us passionately against the war and those as passionately supportive of it are at hopeless loggerheads and can't really tolerate each other anymore. Happily, our people far outnumber the other side, and are expanding day by day.

After an hour or two at Rockefeller Center, we decided to march to the Times Square recruiting center and continue reading. As I walked all the way down the vigil line to request that people follow me there, I was struck by the diversity of the group—not just grannies, but men, younger people and a couple of kids. Even a celebrity or two. I noticed among the many grim faces that of the magnificent Kathleen Chalfant, whom I had recently seen play the lead in the original theatrical production of *Wit*. At Times Square, we stood for another hour or more reading the names of our fallen soldiers and tolling the mournful meditation bell. As I remember, it was drizzling a bit.

We learned later that there were many similar vigils and commemorations for the three thousand GIs all over the United States. We got quite a lot of television and newspaper coverage for our event, as did others, and hoped thereby that we had achieved the desired effect of arousing the public to new or renewed outrage.

The day of our vigil, two more American soldiers died in Iraq.

— *Chapter 15* —

100 Grannies Descend on 100 Senators

Grandmas, get offa your butts
fight against those Medicare cuts
demonstrate against the war
make a stink they can't ignore
—from the song "Grannies, Let's Unite"

Busy Bees and Gout

DESPITE THE POSITIVE COVERAGE we received for our special January 2 vigil, I still felt we had to do something more. The first session of the 110th Congress was due to convene on January 4 and the noises emanating from that newly elected body were not encouraging. We sensed a wavering about the war, a lack of resolve to fulfill the people's mandate to end it with dispatch as exemplified in the recent election, and we realized we had to do something dramatic to try and put some steel in legislators' spines.

It was crisis time—this was probably our best opportunity to bring an end to the occupation. If we waited, Congress would have deals and compromises already locked up that couldn't be easily undone. We saw no alternative other than going to Washington and expressing our urgent concerns directly to all the lawmakers from every state and asking them to join with us. It would be important to have not only impressive numbers but also people representative of the entire nation. This would not be easy, we knew, especially as we would have to solicit volunteer grannies in states far away where the costs and time involved in going to D.C. would be largely prohibitive.

The Grannies spent a lot of time picking the date. There were many considerations—we could not go on Fridays and weekends when Congress would probably not be in session; not too early in January before the new people had their offices and staffs set up; not too late after they'd already made significant resolutions and votes we hoped to influence. We also had to select a day when we would not be competing with other protest groups nor with a huge demonstration planned for the end of the month. We believed that our being grandmothers would resonate in a special way with our elected officials and we wanted to ensure that the focus would remain on us while we were there. Crossing our fingers, we chose Thursday, January 18, for our descent on the Capitol.

We began the huge task of organizing the Washington trip. Although the House was scheduled to make the first vote on a war resolution, we decided to visit just the Senate. We planned to be there for only one day and didn't see how we could scurry around fast enough and far enough to see all 435 Congress members. It would be difficult enough, we realized, to see 100 senators. At our ages, arthritic legs and hips, sore feet, plus the other maladies of older age made it imperative to not cover too much ground.

Each member of our group was assigned two or three states in which to locate activist antiwar grannies to participate. Incidentally, by this time, the Granny Peace Brigade had expanded beyond the original eighteen arrestees. Some, such as Phyllis Cunningham, for instance, had been with us from the beginning and had done everything we had except get arrested. She was essential at the time of our arrest, acting as our liaison to the press and then to the outside world after we were incarcerated. With Phyllis and others now part of us, we had more people to implement our plot to storm the Senate—perhaps twenty-five or thirty Grannies in all.

In addition to reaching out all over the country to find willing grannies, another time-consuming and extremely frustrating task was trying to make appointments with the senators. Given that we only had a few weeks to accomplish this massive job, we had to really knock ourselves out. The Grannies' fax machines were going full blast as we sent letter after letter to Senate offices. We phoned Washington constantly and our phone bills exploded. Unfortunately, all that effort produced limited results: we managed to get some appointments with staff members but almost none with their bosses.

Another crucial problem was picking a spot for our press conference. I wrote to some of the senators known to be strongly opposed to the Iraq debacle, such as Senators Feingold and Kennedy, in an effort to find someone among them who would be willing to join us at our press meeting. At least one was vital to the plan. Press conferences were not permitted inside the Capitol or Senate Office Building unless one were holding one with a senator or a congressperson. The alternatives were not satisfactory—groups could meet outdoors at the Capitol in certain locations, but we were worried about the tricks January weather could play on us, plus meeting at another facility away from the Senate's home base would most likely have discouraged media attention. Try as I might, nobody responded to my requests. What to do? Without the all-important press conference, we couldn't make the clamor necessary to have an impact on the public, or, for that matter, probably, Capitol Hill itself.

Our good pal, Judge Frank Barbaro, came to our rescue

at the last minute. He steered me to Dennis Kucinich, whose 2006 presidential campaign he had run in Brooklyn. Although Kucinich was not a senator but a congressman (D-Ohio), he agreed to appear with us and arranged for us to hold our press event in the Capitol Building. Whew . . . I breathed a big sigh of relief. The whole event would have been derailed without Congressman Kucinich's help.

I looked forward eagerly to the conference. It was hard to estimate how many grandmother-activists would be in Washington in total, but judging from the response we got through our outreach, we calculated we'd have somewhere around one hundred. It was an exciting prospect I certainly didn't want to miss. I began packing my stuff Tuesday in preparation for going to D.C. the next day. We wanted to be there in time for a six p.m. dinner on Wednesday evening, January 17, at the Stewart Mott House, for a meet-and-greet with all the women arriving from other states, many of whom we had never met. We had chosen the Mott House, as it is known, because of its legendary beauty, its proximity to the action center of Washington, and, most of all, because it was free to those involved in liberal causes, due to a legacy of Mr. Mott, a progressive philanthropist.

During the day on Tuesday, I noticed my big toe was bothering me. It grew worse and worse and, by Tuesday night, the throbbing was practically unbearable. I had to confront the reality that it was too painful for me to consider traveling. I figured it was another attack of gout, which I had suffered once before, and I knew it wouldn't go away by itself. Reluctantly, I notified the "girls" that I wouldn't be able to accompany them and asked Bob Sann and Fran Sears to handle the press. I had already prepared a supply of press packs, which they picked up. With great disappointment, but with total confidence in their ability to handle the job, I bade them well.

Grannies Storm the Senate

Luckily, I got full reports from many of the Grannies and lots of pictures, and so am able to give a fairly comprehensive account of what occurred at the Senate on January 18, 2007. Has there ever been another occasion where so many grannies from all over America, some in their eighties and nineties, some in wheelchairs, some with canes, some legally blind and legally deaf, converged on the Capitol to press their concerns and lobby every single senator or a staffperson? It was historic, to say the least.

The determined women arrived at the Capitol before nine A.M. at the security check facility, where they waited outside for about forty-five minutes while their names were verified. It was very cold, and some of the elderly protesters were in wheelchairs or hanging on to walkers. Some of the less handicapped pleaded with the guards to at least let the disabled women wait inside until their names were checked, but the guards refused. It's apparent that disregard of the elderly starts before you even get into the hallowed halls where the lawmakers take (inadequate) care of the people's business!

At the press conference, Congressman Kucinich spoke eloquently about the need to get out of Iraq and applauded the Grannies for being what he called "the conductors on the train of peace." We feel that if we're the conductors, he certainly is the engineer—he has boldly opposed this shameful war from the beginning and been consistently vocal in his opposition. On January 15, he presented a plan for exiting Iraq that the Granny Peace Brigade fully supported. Newly elected Maryland congressman Albert Wynn also appeared at the press meeting and spoke passionately about the need to bring the occupation to an early conclusion. Strongly antiwar congresswoman Barbara Lee of California was able to make a brief stop-by on her way to a meeting.

Another eloquent speaker was the heroic Ann Wright, representing Hawaii. Ann, a former army reserves colonel and diplomat, resigned her diplomatic post in protest the day before "Shock and Awe" was launched. Since then, she has been a tireless advocate for bringing the troops home without delay. Before joining the Grannies in Washington, she had been in Cuba, where she investigated conditions at Guantánamo. Ann travels the globe constantly on behalf of the peace movement.

Also speaking was Geoff Millard, a member of Iraq Veterans Against the War, who later accompanied the Grannies on their rounds and was described by them as "highly articulate and knowledgeable" and of great help as they'd presented their demands and argued their case.

The Grannies were all moved to tears by the words of Elaine Johnson, who had lost her son in Iraq. Elaine came to Washington from South Carolina, and we are so grateful to her for sharing her tragic story with us. She is a committed member of Gold Star Families for Peace.

A highlight of the press conference was feisty 92-year-old Marie Runyon who, in her usual outrageously amusing style, told the room what she thought of George W. Bush. Although Marie is both legally blind and deaf, she considers these conditions mere inconveniences and goes everywhere and does everything, anyhow.

Also speaking was the New York Granny Peace Brigade "celebrity," our Broadway actress/playwright and great-grandmother, Vinie Burrows.

The women then fanned out in teams to meet with all the senators or their staff, to give them white roses attached by a black ribbon to a card saying, "We will not be silent," the theme for the Granny Peace Brigade; the Granny "12 Points of Peace" demands; and a copy of George McGovern's fine book, *Out of Iraq*. They were able to secure face-to-face meet-

> *"When people ask me, 'Do you think your actions*
> *make any difference?' I answer 'YES!' because*
> *we became the voices of those who wanted to, but*
> *for some reason couldn't speak out. Because one*
> *person makes a difference."*
> —Judy Lear

ings with a few senators and congresspeople, but mostly met with staff—not surprising, it is supposed, given the enormous numbers of meetings on Capitol Hill that day.

However, the Grannies were able to grab a few senators for direct interchanges. The New Jersey faction met with their very receptive senators, Frank R. Lautenberg and Robert Menendez, both opponents of the Iraq War. Mr. Menendez had opposed the original resolution authorizing George Bush to conduct a preemptive war on Iraq. Mr. Lautenberg had not been in the Senate at that time but has been a consistent opponent of the Iraq disaster. The New Jersey grandmothers were very impressed with the exhibit outside his Senate office, which shows pictures of every fallen military man and woman who was a casualty in Iraq.

Gold Star Mother Elaine Johnson had a lengthy meeting with her South Carolina senator, Republican Jim DeMint, who agreed that it was time for the troops to come home. He said that they were giving Bush one more chance (it is assumed he meant the "Surge") but if that didn't work, they would take action. He was very kind to Elaine, and she was most pleased: she had a personal situation for which she requested his assistance, and he immediately offered help; in fact, his aides called her the next day to begin the process.

Other senators and House members with whom some

Philadelphia grannies had face-to-face meetings were Senator Arlen Specter (R-PA) and Pennsylvania representative Chaka Fattah from Philadelphia, who told the Philly women, "I'm on your side." Also, some of the New Yorkers had a very cordial meeting with Rep. Charlie Rangel, now head of the powerful House Ways and Means Committee, who knows the New York Granny Peace Brigade well, has supported them in many ways in the past, and offered on that Thursday to give them a substantial monetary contribution. A few of the women had a brief encounter in the hall with Nancy Pelosi as she was scurrying to open the Congress, during which she praised the grannies for their peace work.

For the most part, however, the lobbying group met with assistants and advisers. Debbie Hardy, who came from Ohio to join the Grannies, met with aides to Sen. George V. Voinovich, Sen. Sherrod Brown and Rep. John Boehner, all representing Ohio, and with Sen. Patrick Leahy of Vermont, and asked three questions formulated by her son, Jeremy Brooks: (1) In your opinion, what needs to happen before we can begin withdrawing American troops? (2) Do you support a deadline for the Iraqi government to start taking control of the security of Iraq? (3) If the situation in Iraq does not improve after we send in additional troops, at what point in time would you suggest to the president that enough is enough? Each of the Ohio representatives *did* send her their answers, and suggested that the questions be asked of *all* senators. Debbie spoke to their staff about her missing husband, Qassim Flayah Ubead, an Iraqi policeman she had met while he was assigned to the United States for training in a police academy, so he could return to Iraq and teach antiterrorism in the Baghdad Police Academy. He disappeared in Iraq in October 2005 and Debbie has been desperately searching for him ever since. She hasn't found him or learned of his fate but has never given up the search. She has visited Jordan and

Syria to seek information, and plans to go to Iraq in early 2008.

Generally, the Grannies were treated with respect and, for the most part, felt they had made a significant impact. The New York delegation, for instance, had a very cordial meeting with Senator Schumer's aides, who listened attentively and had a give-and-take with them that was quite satisfactory.

A few of the visitors came across Senator John McCain in the Capitol rotunda as he was holding an impromptu press conference. They listened politely as he ranted on about the need for more troops, about how we must respect George Bush, and so on, and then followed him as he walked back to his office. Laurie Arbeiter approached him as he was about to enter his domain and asked, "How did you feel when Bush nullified your torture amendment, using the signing statement? What did Iraq have to do with 9/11? Justify the illegal invasion."

McCain said, "I appreciate your views."

Laurie answered, "You do *not* appreciate our views."

"I *do* appreciate your views," McCain insisted.

"No, you *don't* appreciate our views," she countered. "How could you support the administration policies regarding Iraq, if you did?" at which point McCain quickly ducked into his office.

As cordial as their meeting with Sen. Schumer's staff had been, most of the New York delegation were disappointed with their meeting with Hillary Clinton's people. The women had been shunted for fifteen or twenty minutes through the halls and up and down steps, as the staff sought a bigger room in which to hold the meeting. This was hard on some of the older women, and, once there, the person with whom they were to meet, Hillary's chief policy advisor, Laurie Rubiner, kept them waiting. This left them with a sense they were disrespected and that their opinions were of no consequence.

Mortified by the way they were being treated, some of the Grannies expressed intense animosity toward Ms. Rubiner. One blurted, for instance, "If Hillary Clinton runs for president, I could never support her." The antagonistic attitude of some of the Grannies greatly bothered a few others, who felt embarrassed by such blatant hostility to their hostess. During the course of the meeting, Ms. Rubiner's body language changed from accepting to defensive as the Grannies made their points. When the Grannies interrupted her rhetoric with actual facts about Senator Clinton's stances, Ms. Rubiner had no adequate response. Late in the meeting, the women questioned Ms. Rubiner as to why nobody on her staff seemed to be taking notes, which prompted one of the aides to finally begin doing so.

At the end of the meeting, Ms. Rubiner said to Iraq vet Geoff Millard, "I'm proud of your service." He asked, "Which service—my tour of duty in Iraq or my service in the antiwar movement?" "Your service in Iraq," she replied. Geoff said, "If you knew what I did, you would not be so proud." Geoff was not proud of himself for participating in an illegal war. "I'm still proud of your service," was her answer, totally missing the point—just as Hillary has continually missed the point about the wrongness of the Iraq occupation. The Grannies didn't feel they'd made any significant impact on Hillary that day, vis à vis the Iraq war.

After completing their arduous lobbying through the long, long corridors of the Capitol and the various office buildings, the grannies gathered at 4 P.M. in the atrium of the Hart Building. At first, they softly read aloud the First Amendment and then intoned quietly the names of the fallen soldiers with a gentle meditation bell sound at the end of each name. As they augmented the volume of their voices, the Capitol police approached and said that they had better stop the ringing of the bell and lower their voices, that they were "disturbing the peace." One of the grandmothers said to him, "You are concerned that our reading the names of the dead is disturbing the peace? The peace has already been disturbed by some of the people that work in this building. We are here to *restore* the peace."

Although I had sent out a lot of press releases before the Granny Descent and even sent one from my sickbed on the day of their visit to the Senate, very little American press showed up to the gathering. There were some journalists and cameras from foreign countries but, all in all, an event of this great significance and, in my view, of compelling public interest, did not get the coverage it deserved. But we like to think that it was a big buzz, not a big bust, in the legislative branch! ⌒

— Chapter 16 —

The McCain Mutiny

Grandmas, let's unite
while we are still upright
let's protest that parasite
Watch out! We've just begun to fight!
    —from the song "Grannies, Let's Unite"

Serenading the Senator

NOTHING WE OR ANYBODY ELSE DID stopped the war. More
and more blood was being shed, and we wondered: Why is
our government still sending our kids to die? Why are we
allowing it to happen? When will Congress stop this slaughter? Isn't there something that can be done? We imagined
those poor young kids of ours boldly patrolling an area of
Baghdad or maybe Fallujah, strong and brave, maybe laughing with one another, and then, boom, they are gone—in pieces.
Perhaps some of them don't die immediately but lie there in
agony, calling out their mother's name.

If the war is still going on when this narrative reaches your
eyes, I hope what you've read here will compel you to action—perhaps to call your senator, maybe to write a letter to
your local newspaper, or, if you're in New York City, to attend my Wednesday vigil. *We simply must put an end to this*
useless, doomed horror.

One of the chief proponents of the "surge" is, as you all know, Senator John McCain. A man of incredible courage who endured years of torture as a Vietnamese prisoner of war. A man who fought hard against the Establishment to put an end to campaign financing misdeeds. A maverick, really, who seemed to have a real independent streak and whom even Democrats trusted to follow his conscience for the benefit of us all.

And then, he seemed to lose his judgment. Did all the years of torture unhinge him mentally in some way, I wonder? I would have expected that he would employ common sense and moral conviction and oppose the bombing and occupation of Iraq, particularly in view of the fact that he owed George W. Bush no loyalty. After all, the president had attacked him viciously when they were both vying for the Republican nomination for president. Instead, though, the senator supported Bush's war. And, more than that, he has been urging that many more thousands of our precious youngsters be deployed to Iraq. He called for an even greater increase in troop numbers than President Bush had originally asked for.

Some of the grannies had already confronted McCain during their day in Washington, and now we had another opportunity to tell him what we thought of his positions. We planned a sneak attack for his visit to the Big Apple on February 27, 2007. This came about through our dear Malachy McCourt, who e-mailed me that he had heard McCain would be in New York City that day to speak to the Irish American Republicans Club meeting to be held at the Women's National Republican Club. McCourt asked if I might gather a few of the grandmothers together to join him in a protest there.

The timing was perfect. The Women's National Republican Club was a block away from my Rockefeller Center vigil, and McCain's speech was scheduled on the same day. I knew the building well, as I had attended meetings of the New York Sheet Music Society, a group composed of mostly songwriters, which meets there. You can imagine the twinges of guilt I felt on those occasions from being in enemy territory, but I must say it is a beautiful mansion—right off Fifth Avenue on West 51st Street, prime real estate indeed. A group from my vigil decided to go hassle him.

I performed my by-now practically automatic task of sending out press advisories to my ever-growing list of press and media contacts, and we began to prepare for our slightly mischievous action. Malachy dreamed up what I considered a terrific slogan, "Need a surge, McCain? Try Viagra," and I asked one of our artist Grannies, Ann Shirazi, to make a sign with that intriguingly naughty line.

After our Wednesday vigil, thirty or forty of us, including our regular Veterans for Peace platoon, formed a line outside the Women's National Republican Club. Police officers were clustered around the building entrance, and they insisted that we move across the street to hold our demonstration. We did so, and the cops put up an iron fence to keep us dangerous old grandmothers and elderly veterans of World War II, Korea, and Vietnam penned in, so we couldn't pose any perilous threat to the senator and his entourage.

While we waited for McCain to appear—and it was a long, long wait—we shouted our antiwar catchwords and sang our peace songs. At one point, Malachy sang, a capella, in his rich and booming voice, "Johnny, I Hardly Knew Ya." I had heard

> "A love for education and the arts is one of the greatest gifts a parent or grandparent can instill."
> —Nydia Leaf

him sing this heartbreaking piece one other time before I knew him, at a Freedom Follies show produced by Theaters Against War (THAW), when I was mesmerized and moved to tears, as was the entire audience, by his highly dramatic and powerful rendition. Remember, Malachy is a professional Broadway, television, and film actor in addition to all his other assets, and a really fine one. I think if Bush could hear Malachy McCourt sing that deeply affecting ballad, it might turn even *his* indifferent heart around and he'd stop murdering our young military. The lyrics may be the most moving ones of all in the antiwar song repertoire and go right to the core of the tragedy of war.

Johnny, I hardly Knew Ya

(to tune of "When Johnny Comes Marching Home Again")

While going the road to sweet Athy, taroo, taroo
While going the road to sweet Athy, taroo, taroo
While going the road to sweet Athy
a stick in my hand and a tear in my eye
A doleful damsel I heard cry
Johnny, I hardly knew ya

CHORUS:
With drums and guns and guns and drums, haroo, haroo
with drums and guns and guns and drums, haroo, haroo
with drums and guns and guns and drums
the enemy nearly slew ya,
my darling dear you look so queer,
Johnny, I hardly knew ya

Where are the eyes that looked so mild, haroo, haroo
Where are the eyes that looked so mild, haroo, haroo

Where are the eyes that looked so mild,
When my poor heart you first beguiled,
Why did you skedaddle from me and the child,
Johnny, I hardly knew ya

Where are the legs with which you run, haroo, haroo
Where are the legs with which you run, haroo, haroo
Where are the legs with which you run
When you went off to shoulder a gun
Indeed your dancing days are done,
Johnny, I hardly knew ya

You haven't an arm and you haven't a leg, haroo, haroo
You haven't an arm and you haven't a leg, haroo, haroo
You haven't an arm and you haven't a leg,
You're an eyeless, noseless, chickenless egg
You'll have to be put in a bowl to beg,
Johnny, I hardly knew ya

This final verse was added in his own words by Malachy:

They'll never take our boys again, haroo, haroo
They'll never take our boys again, haroo, haroo
They'll never take our boys again
to turn them into fighting men
Johnny, I swear it to ya

Malachy captivated the crowd with his wit, charm, and gift of gab. He can instantly coin a bon mot on any subject faster than you can say "blarney." He is such a beloved character that some of the police "protecting" McCain from us chatted with him frequently (he showed me his special badge identifying him as the father of a cop—legitimate, to be sure), and even members of the Irish American Republicans Club crossed the street to converse with their adversarial pal on the other side of their political fence.

While we waited for the senator to appear, I was happy to note a number of journalists and TV and still cameramen snapping our pictures and interviewing us, paying particular attention to our risqué sign. After our vigil of about two hours or so, a big black limo pulled up across the street and out stepped the great man. Earlier that day, he had announced his candidacy on *The David Letterman Show*, and seemed to be in an ebullient mood. He turned and waved at us with a big smile on his face, then headed inside. The unexpected had happened. Is it possible John McCain mistook us for fans? Maybe so, but, in any case, *we* felt better. It's always wise to not bottle up feelings of anger. We had needed to vent. The senator got his just deserts: his poll ratings tanked drastically for some time afterward, most likely a direct link to his absolute refusal to back down about Iraq. I like to think that he *did* recognize that we were a bunch of protesters and that we gave him a taste of New York Granny chutzpah. An experience not to be missed!

— Chapter 17 —

A Daring Venture—The Endless War Memorial

We must curse our common fate
When useless war goes on and on
We must pause to commemorate
All those who sadly now are gone
    —from the song "For Those Who Are Lost"

Chasing Celebrities

HAVING TACKLED MCCAIN, now we needed to tackle the Bush regime on a much more sweeping scale. With casualties rising alarmingly and no end in sight, we wracked our brains for an imaginative action that would stimulate the media and thereby prod the public and Congress to action. Laurie Arbeiter proposed a truly innovative happening, to be called the Endless War Memorial. As a lead-in to the fourth anniversary of the war on March 17, 2007, Laurie suggested we read, nonstop, the names of those who had died in Iraq—including American military, Iraqi civilians, coalition members, and journalists. After much debate and occasional friction, the agenda was set. We would gather at the Times Square recruiting station from March 10 through March 16 and hold uninterrupted readings from daybreak to nightfall.

This was a very tricky project to organize. A method was arranged whereby we would solicit people to sign up for fifteen-minute or half-hour shifts at specific times and on specific days, so that the names would be read continuously without any breaks. We contacted every person and group we could think of to invite to participate in this unique event. A couple of stalwart volunteers, Joan Pleune, one of the Granny Peace Brigade's most active members, and Tresa Martinez, a young NYU student we hired temporarily to help coordinate the event, were the principal people responsible for scheduling people's appointments, definitely no small chore.

To get good media coverage, I realized I'd have to get celebrities to read the names of war dead. I approached Barbara Barrie, who had spoken at my original rally in 2003 at the Eleanor Roosevelt Statue, and she agreed to join us. Nydia Leaf's friend, Constance Dondore, invited her step-grandson, Liev Schreiber, and he gave us a thumbs-up. Since he had just been acclaimed in a *New York Times* review as the "finest American theater actor of his generation," for his performance on Broadway in *Talk Radio*, we were quite thrilled that he would be part of our memorial event. Jenny Heinz secured an enthusiastic yes from her good friend, actress Kathleen Chalfant, who was starring in the Broadway production, *Spalding Grey: Stories Left to Tell*. Marie Runyon contacted her old friend Ruby Dee. Our pal Malachy McCourt also came on board.

I pulled out all the stops, including writing personal letters to every star currently appearing or rehearsing in a Broadway and Off-Broadway play, and had the missives delivered to them at their stage door. My list included Frank Langella, Vanessa Redgrave, Christopher Plummer, and Angela Lansbury, to name a few. I was disappointed that we had no response at first, but one night I got a telephone call from Mary Louise

Wilson, one of the two leads in *Grey Gardens*, saying she would like to read and telling me her available time.

In the meantime, Nydia wrote to the cast of *Journey's End* and invited them. This was extremely significant because it is a play about World War 1 and depicts the horror and futility of war, concluding with the deaths of all the soldiers characterized, and it was therefore very appropriate that the actors recite the names of our current war dead. A number of Grannies, including me, had seen the play and were absolutely overwhelmed with its power and brilliance. We were very pleased when one of the players, Jefferson Mays, accepted our request.

I was encouraged by the response we'd received, but we needed a superstar to pull it all together. I was too aware of the problems of getting the media to come out for one's event without a really huge "name" or a beguiling gimmick. I went after Oscar winner Susan Sarandon, so noted for her liberal activism, along with that of her partner, Tim Robbins. I was able to locate the person who handled her scheduling and, after a series of e-mails defining exactly what she would do, she complied with our appeal. I was soon to learn the enormous difference between "superstar" and "well known."

I thought long and hard about how to handle the press situation with different big-name people coming at different times on different days. Presumably, it was customary to have just one opening-day press conference for an occasion like this, but since our main attraction, Susan Sarandon, would be attending on the second day, this presented problems as how to best seduce the press into covering our event. Further complicating matters was the fact that our other boldface names were scheduled for yet other days. Finally, I got the idea of holding our opening press conference on the first day, Sunday, March 10, per usual, and then sending a press release each day to announce who would be participating on the following day and at what time. It was unconventional, I assumed, but necessary—just like the Grannies' entire antiwar effort.

I wasn't able to get the show-biz luminaries for the opening press conference, although Congressman Charlie Rangel and other local politicians agreed to come. I scheduled it for noon and started putting press kits together.

Attacks of the Heart and Other Calamities

I was quite excited as I awaited Sunday's beginning of our Endless War Memorial and meeting with the media, and hardly slept Saturday night. But, as certain people, most memorably our departed secretary of defense, Rumsfeld, have been known to say, "Stuff happens." In this case, the stuff started early Sunday morning, when I heard moans coming from my living room. I went out there to discover my live-in companion, Herb, in great pain, sweating slightly and a little bit incoherent. He just didn't look right to me. He was having pains in his back, his upper arms, and his jaw, but not at all in his chest. The jaw was the alarming symptom to me, as my mother had had jaw pain when she'd suffered angina years before. He had been having these pains for a few weeks, but they'd always go away if he sat down for a few minutes. He told me that this time they had lasted for over an hour and hadn't dissipated. Although Herb hates hospitals and ordinarily would insist I not call 911, he allowed me to do so this time, and soon the EMS people arrived to take him to Roosevelt Hospital's nearby emergency room.

I met Herb when I was 25 and he was 32. Wow, was he something—tall, dark and handsome—as well as a very fine clarinet player. At that stage of my life, I would only date musicians, and he fit the bill nicely. He also was gentlemanly, witty, and always looked as if he'd stepped out of the pages of *Gentleman's Quarterly*. In other words, he was perfect. Ah, if I'd had the good sense to recognize it. We had a brief fling, but then I fluffed him off on a girlfriend soon after we started seeing each other, because he was too "square" for my then offbeat sensibilities. I went on to marry another man named Herb, and had two children, divorced, remarried briefly, then had a number of other relationships. Every ten years or so, Herb Hecsh would contact me and we'd resume our romance, but briefly. On the other two or three occasions when we got together, it was he who dumped me, as I recall.

I hadn't seen or heard from him for about ten years when I got a telephone call from Herb saying he would like to see me. I was then 65, and had more or less shut down romantically. I stalled for a few months until I could lose some excess weight, and finally agreed for him to come to New York from Philadelphia, where he was living, for a weekend visit. I worried a lot about what he would look like at his age, 72, thinking he probably had gotten fat and bald. To my pleasant surprise, however, he was still very good looking and trim, only white haired. This time, it all clicked for us, and I felt like a teenager again. I was quite surprised to be in love at my age. And this time, he didn't dump me—I guess he was now too old and probably lonely to continue the quest for the elusive Ms. Right and that whatever had turned him off in earlier years was no longer an issue. After a short while, we decided to live together. That was more than ten years ago. He has been a wonderful helpmate and, thank God, shares my political beliefs. When I broke my leg a few years ago, he took care of me as a mother would tend her child, and was equally solicitous and helpful during my recuperation from hip replacement surgery almost five years ago.

We got Herb to the ER but they couldn't seem to figure out what was wrong. By then, he was feeling a little better and, since he was in the capable hands of the hospital staff, I felt secure about running over to the noon press conference, which was nearby. Naturally, I felt frantic because I felt my presence was essential: I had put it together and knew who had been invited. So, full of frenzy and also guilt at leaving Herb, I dashed over to Times Square.

On the little recruiting station cement traffic island on Broadway at 44th Street, I found a beautiful space created by our Grannies and a group of artists calling themselves the Critical Voice. There was a small platform with a microphone in front of it. two people were standing on the platform, reading names. Next to them was a person who clinked the meditation bell after each name, age, rank, and date of death was announced. Flowers adorned the site, everywhere were symbols relating to the ongoing war: a pair of children's shoes side by side with a pair of American combat boots . . . a triangularly folded American flag, the kind given to families of fallen soldiers, placed on a chair . . . above and behind them, a big banner stating "We will not be silent," in English and in Arabic, and an enormous photograph of grieving Iraqi women. Our reading space was set up so that people watching it could see the recruiting center in the background, with its never-ending film showing soldiers training while looking blissfully happy. A very ironic juxtaposition, as in front of the readers' platform was a full-size casket covered with an American flag and a full-length photograph of a beautiful young marine in full dress uniform, lying in an open coffin. His name was Alex Arredondo; he had been killed at the age of 20 on his second tour of duty in Iraq. In front of the casket, his father, Carlos, had placed a number of white crosses representing all the other young soldiers who died needlessly for Bush's psychotic compulsion to be a macho man. It was impossible to look at the casket without being emotionally overcome, and the tears flowed from my eyes.

I proceeded with the press conference, which was not particularly well attended, then rushed back to the hospital, determined to send out another press advisory later on announcing Susan Sarandon's scheduled appearance the next day. I found Herb still hanging around the emergency room, still with no diagnosis. One doctor thought he might have had a mild heart attack, another didn't. But a lovely young Korean-American cardiologist, Bette Kim, came on the scene, examined him and listened intently to an account of his symptoms, and she decided to keep him overnight and perform a heart catheterization the next day, suspecting he had three, possibly four blocked arteries. When he was admitted and settled into a room, I felt free to go home and attend to my press advisory.

But I was in for another sneak attack, although not by any means on the same level of crisis as Herb's medical condition. When I attempted to turn on my computer, nothing happened. After trying a number of little operations, I had to conclude that it had died—and with it all my notes, files, and documents. Whew, what a blow! My immediate problem was to get out my announcement about Susan Sarandon, and achieve better press coverage than we'd had the first day. I called around looking to borrow a computer, with no luck. Somebody suggested going to Kinko's to rent their computer, which I did late that night. I spent a sleepless, anxious night worrying about Herb, about the press turnout, and about getting a functional computer. Clearly, this was not one of my better days.

> *"Get to meet and spend time living with or at least talking with people from societies and cultures other than one's own—study and vacation groups, for example. You will really like some and not others but you will not want any to have their families, their homes and their homelands destroyed."*
> —**Barbara Walker**

Mourning in Times Square

The next morning, I returned to our little shrine in the middle of Times Square. The continuous reading was in progress, of course, and promptly at noon Susan Sarandon appeared dressed in a smart black leather pants suit, looking slim and lovely and far younger than her 60 years. There was a solid semicircle of cameras and reporters covering every inch of space in front of her. We had set up her reading so that she shared it with Kathleen Chalfant. Iraqi names were read along with English ones, Kathleen reciting those in Arabic and Susan, those in English. The two women read for about half an hour, cameras flashing constantly throughout. Then Susan suddenly started to leave the area to get to a car. That's when I learned the difference between a superstar and a mere famous person. As she turned away, all the reporters and cameramen ran after her in a rush and swarmed around her so that she couldn't move. They interviewed her and interviewed her and took picture after picture. They all but ignored Kathleen, a theater and television actress very familiar to the theatrically literate, but not a superstar. I almost felt sorry for her.

I then hurried to the hospital to see how Herb was doing. The catheterization had indeed showed four blocked arteries, and Dr. Kim recommended that Herb have a quadruple bypass as soon as possible. They moved him uptown to a sister hospital, St Luke's, with top heart surgeons and, the next morning, he was operated on. I wasn't able to get back to the Endless War Memorial because the second hospital was far away and it was important that I be with Herb every day.

Apparently, I missed some highly dramatic events. Carlos Arredondo brought the coffin intermittently throughout the week. Everybody read—Iraq war veterans, grieving Gold Star families, grannies, kids, foreigners, and all the celebrities we had invited except Barbara Barrie, whose husband had recently died. Amy Goodman read. Kathleen Chalfant came back two more times with her husband, Henry, to read again. Former congresswoman of Watergate fame Liz Holtzman read. The great Ruby Dee, now in her eighties, came to Times Square to read. Our Vinie Burrows read. Altogether, over four hundred readers were there, and never a moment's lull. Naturally, we couldn't find names for all the Iraqis who've been killed in the war. Complete records aren't kept, and some estimates place the total at 650,000, so we proclaimed that each Iraqi name we recited represented two hundred others.

One day, an Iraqi woman, Namaa Alward, came to the read-in. A singer-actress, Namaa had been a political refugee in Egypt for a number of years but returned to Iraq in 2003 to be a human shield in an effort, along with others, to prevent the invasion. She lost many family members and friends in the occupation of Iraq. When she and Carlos Arredondo met at the Memorial, they embraced in shared grief, both tragic victims of our American violation.

On the fourth day of the reading, a thin, young Iraqi boy, about twelve, showed up, wanting to get one of our T-shirts emblazoned with our theme, in Arabic and English, "We will not be silent." He stood next to two men arguing the merits and demerits of the war. One of them, a very big guy who was defending the U.S. occupation of Iraq, said such things as, "It's a good thing we took out Saddam Hussein. He went into people's houses in the middle of the night and dragged people out," and other comments justifying our country's attack. As the small boy listened to the man, he began to get visibly upset. Finally, he literally leapt in the air, pointed his finger at the huge man, and cried "Liar, liar" and began to cry. The man dismissed the kid, saying, "Oh, he's a Baathist," and turned away. The Grannies hugged and comforted the child as best they could. As he left, they urged him to return.

Friday, the last day of the readings, swooped in with a hail of rain, sleet, and snow, wind blowing fiercely, a setting worthy of Shakespeare's *The Tempest*. During the readings, the Grannies became aware of a small figure standing nearby. It was the Iraqi boy who had wanted the T-shirt. He said to Laurie, who had given him the shirt, "Miss, I've never known Americans who care, Americans like all of you. I lost my good friend, and for what? War is not good, miss." Then, shivering, he unzipped his woefully skimpy jacket and proudly displayed the T-shirt the grannies had given him. The people who had prepared and operated the memorial felt that everything they had endured for six long days—the difficult organizing, the constant standing, braving the elements—was well worth it for that poignant moment alone.

For those of you wondering what happened to Herb, despite the fact that open heart surgery is probably one of the most traumatic of all surgeries, Herb came through it okay. He had a long and uncomfortable recuperation but, after about seven weeks, began to be fairly functional and now is pretty much back to normal.

Unfortunately, the computer didn't recover but, thanks to the generosity of the Granny Peace Brigade, I was able to replace it. ⌒

— *Chapter 18* —

I Share the Stage with Susan Sarandon

> *Mirror, mirror on the wall*
> *Who's the fairest of them all?*
> *I know for sure that it's not me*
> *I've still got eyes, I still can see!*
> —from the song "Where'd I Go?"

I GOT A CALL FROM MICHAEL FLYNN, the professor at York College in Queens who had invited Carol Husten and me to address his class the summer of 2006. He asked me if I'd be on a panel March 23 at John Jay College, another of his teaching places, to discuss women in the antiwar movement. He said Amy Goodman, the revered radio journalist, and Susan Sarandon would be my copanelists.

Moi? Sharing a platform with two such exalted personages, one a peacenik goddess, the other a film goddess? It seemed unreal. I have done my bit for the peace movement but haven't the name or prestige to qualify for such illustrious company. However, anything to spread the Granny Gospel!

"How the heck am I going to command any attention when all eyes are on these celebrated women? Particularly superstar Susan. What person in the audience with intact sanity would want to listen to or look at *me* with gorgeous Ms. Sarandon to stare at?" I asked myself. "Well, I can't even begin to seize the spotlight. I'll just have to give the best yet brief speech I'm capable of and then sneak off to the sidelines," I thought.

The day arrived. Now, what would *you* wear if you were 75 years old, overweight, hadn't shopped for new clothes for approximately ten years, and were about to sit right next to Susan Sarandon? Black, right? Black jacket, black pants. Hide the bod and then hope they don't notice.

I arrived while another panel discussion was in progress. There was Professor this and Professor that, deified experts with degrees three miles long. I wish I could remember what they discussed, but I was so nervous and felt so outclassed that my brain must have frozen. I can't remember a single thing about the panel discussion except I hoped it would never end so I wouldn't have to go up on that same stage and make a fool of myself.

A lunch break was finally called that preceded my part of the program. I picked at my lunch and tried to pass the time by reading the flier for the forum, which listed all the impressive participants with their fancy titles, the books they'd authored, the awards they'd garnered. None of this did much to bolster my sagging confidence, which was now about to hit the floor.

The time came when I had no choice but to go up to the dais. I sat there alone, waiting for the two notables who were scheduled to join me. They didn't come, but the audience did. I was told that both Susan and Amy were delayed. Oh,

> "There is always a good tune left in an old fiddle . . . for the Grannies the tune is trying to make the world a safer place."
> —Carol Husten

dear. I continued to sit there, trying to look commanding and calm while squirming with embarrassment inside.

Finally, Susan arrived and sat down next to me. She looked smashing—I've read someplace that she is 60 years old but, if so, she's the best-looking and youngest-appearing 60-year-old in existence. It seemed to me, furthermore, that she hasn't had plastic surgery. Her face, though youthful and lovely, has just enough lines to establish that she's had a life and isn't trying to hide the fact that she's no longer an ingénue.

Amy Goodman didn't show up at all, so it was agreed that I would speak first, and then Susan was to answer questions from the audience after—no speech. I stood at the lectern and made my speech, in which I outlined the history of the Grandmothers and how they had come into being through my two-person vigil in January 2004 and evolved from there. Now, I've been a performer all my life, practically, in all sorts of situations—in cabarets, on television, in plays, in jazz groups, in concerts, and I've had nervous moments, but nothing like the nervousness I felt that day. I was literally shaking all over, and I could hear it in my voice as I spoke—it quavered. I even felt faint at one point and feared I would pass out. But I got through it and, finally, it was over. I received quite a nice hand from the audience, as a matter of fact. I also vaguely remember introducing about five or six Grannies from the audience.

Then, it was Susan's turn to talk in the form of answering questions. I was stunned. The woman is brilliant. Her answers were so knowledgeable and intelligent, and all delivered with tremendous ease and wit. I couldn't help but be very impressed. She spoke of her travel to a Third World country with a group of activist women. She gave long and thoughtful answers to questions about how a mother can encourage social consciences in her children, and about how much of the critical state of our nation to impart to kids. She discussed how her progressive social activism has impacted her career—not much, as it turned out. She commented that Hollywood was more concerned that older actresses not get fat than what their political leanings were. She was, quite simply, wonderful.

I noticed that as she sat there throughout the discussion, she constantly doodled on a pad of paper. When she left, the doodles remained on our table. To this day, I regret that I didn't have the presence of mind to grab that pad and take it with me. What dark secrets of her psyche would it have revealed? What inner turmoil? (Can a gorgeous, slim, rich, award-winning movie star living with a brilliant, tall, rich, award-winning movie director/actor and progressive hero feel any turmoil?)

As I was leaving the hall, a very attractive man came up and stopped me on my way out. He was a film director directing the C-SPAN videotaping of our seminar that was made that day to be televised later. He said that if he were directing me in a film, he wouldn't tell me a thing, that my delivery was perfect and my writing excellent

Wow!

No, I wasn't acclaimed. I wasn't even important. But I made an impression on someone. His praise made me feel that for a few moments, I *was* acclaimed and important. I am certainly no Susan Sarandon—but, I realized, one must never compare oneself to others. One's accomplishments can only be measured by the progress one makes within one's own limitations. ⌒

— *Chapter 19* —

Cindy's Bombshell Announcement

Get me out of here
Let me have my space
Let me disappear
Without a trace
  —from the song "The Inner Laura Bush"

IN THE SPRING OF 2007, the news came that Cindy Sheehan was retiring from the peace movement. She was exhausted, her health was not good, she was burnt out, and she felt that, in addition to enduring attacks from the Right, she was now also being attacked from the Left. Apparently, there was wide divergence of opinion among liberals and progressives concerning Cindy. Perhaps her advocacy of impeachment was not universally applauded on the Left, and some of her statements regarding other issues may have turned off some in the movement. But I'm not privy to the reasons, and prefer not to speculate. She felt she needed to get back to her three remaining children and be a mother again, and that she had let down her dead son, Casey, by not being able to end the occupation, as she had so valiantly and ceaselessly tried to do.

Although we Grandmothers had begun opposing the war more than a year before she joined us at Rockefeller Center, we only created a minor stir by comparison. When Cindy began her vigil at the Bush ranch, the antiwar movement really exploded into a powerful force. She rocketed to the head of the war opposition and turned it into a gigantic cause célèbre. Where would we be today if not for her? The war is not over, sadly. But, it is Topic A in the presidential campaign, a majority of Americans now want us to pull out of Iraq, and Congress is grappling with ways to end the occupation, although their spines are still too soft to do what's really necessary. I think Cindy Sheehan has had a lot to do with this slowly evolving waking-up of the American people.

One of the last times I saw Cindy was on December 7, 2006, at a Code Pink party in midtown Manhattan. It was held on the top-floor private apartment of the owner of the furniture store occupied by the rest of the building, and it was really something. The living room, where we all assembled, looked like an exotic Arabian house of ill repute—plush sofas and hassocks, big fat embroidered pillows piled in various parts of the room, tassels and Oriental wall hangings and carpets everywhere you looked—spectacular.

I had a few minutes to talk privately with Cindy, and she discussed the hysterectomy she'd had months before, which was an emergency operation in the midst of her camping out at Crawford, Texas. It sounded to me as if she hadn't given herself sufficient time to recuperate before she'd torn back into her frenzy of activity all over the world, and she agreed with me. I was a little concerned but, later that night, ever so slightly tipsy as were the rest of us at the evening's end, she gave a fabulous speech—powerful and poignant and yet hilariously funny at times. She seemed to be in really good shape, and I decided I had nothing to worry about.

Well, I should have worried. Everybody should have worried, most of all Cindy. She's tall and strong looking, but she is just another vulnerable human being, and the stress of losing

> *"Happiness involves closing the distance between*
> *who we are and who we should be."*
> —**Paul Rosa**

her son, poor health, constant travel and speech-making, writing three books while engaged in taxing political protests, and
several incarcerations and trials was doomed to catch up with
her.

I believe the statement she made when she "retired" from
active opposition to the war was a bit impulsive, in that she
seemed to be saying that ending the occupation and changing our government's policies was a hopeless quest and she
was therefore giving up the struggle. The implication, although I know she didn't mean it that way, was that if she,
alone, couldn't conclude the war, then nobody could. What
about the rest of us engaged in the struggle, not on the same
focused level as Cindy for the most part but, nevertheless,
trying? We have to believe that there is hope, otherwise we
would have to retire, also. Obviously, the statement reflected
the exhausted and stressed-out Cindy in a very down moment.

On the day she made her announcement, I heard her interviewed by Amy Goodman on her show *Democracy Now*,
and Cindy sounded much less disheartened. She talked of her
need to restore herself and her connection to her family before going back into the fray in a different way. She talked
of using her "sabbatical" to rethink her strategy and clarify
her priorities. This made perfect sense to me. I think Cindy
did desperately need a long rest to heal the damage to her
body and psyche as much as possible and to regather her en-
ergies for future action. Others would be able to carry on

her heroic fight in the meantime and, though nobody could ever replace her, much could still be accomplished.

I asked Cindy's close friend, Ann Wright, a retired army reserve colonel and former diplomat who gave up her career in the diplomatic corps to devote herself to the cause of ending the war, what her reaction was to Cindy's announcement. Ann, who has traveled often with Cindy and was the commandant, at times, at Camp Casey, had kept in touch with Cindy since she left the movement. Ann feels Cindy was

> expressing the deep frustration we all feel at the Democrats' lack of backbone in pushing legislation to stop funding the war. Cindy feels there can be no compromise when it comes to death. Every day that they allow the war to continue, ten more Americans and one hundred more Iraqis will die. I'm glad that Cindy finally recognized after three years of long and arduous work that she had to take a break. She's had every possible stressful thing happen to her during that time.

As for the Grannies, Lorraine Krofchok, the brilliant and tireless director of Grandmothers for Peace International, spoke very eloquently for all of us in her wise remarks:

> Cindy gave all that she had. She was like a rocket and burned out. I am sure she tried to take on the war and end it by herself—I can empathize with that determination. I, too, take the war personally, but realized I could not stop it by myself, no matter how much I wanted it. It is a huge group effort—sadly, very slow. Once a friend told me that peace making is two steps forward and one step back. We all would like to see things move faster, but they just don't. Our Congress is a disgrace, only looking to 2008 and playing with words. If they stopped the funding and this went "bad," the Demos would be blamed. This way they can "let" Bush continue his war and then point fingers in 2008, while our troops and Iraqis

continue to die. Cindy motivated a lot of people. They must continue. She will always be with us . . .

The wheels of peace turn very, very slowly as we gather more people. Yet, the things we do, those of us here today, we may never see the success of our endeavors. For Grandmothers for Peace, we say, "a better, safer world for the future." We do it not for now but for those to come. (It would be nice, however, if we could see something in our lifetime.) We have to be the continuing embers of hope, never giving up, always being there. We all must remember that silence is affirmation, and we will *not* be silent!

The Grannies greatly appreciated Cindy Sheehan's vast contributions to the peace movement and understood her need to step back, at least for a while. Trying to end the unconscionable Iraq war is essentially a group effort, which must and will go on, with or without her, but hopefully, soon again, with her.

Surprise, surprise! Cindy didn't stay out of the spotlight for long. Almost immediately, she jumped back into the struggle and announced that she was going to oppose Nancy Pelosi for her California congressional seat. Her principal reason for taking such a drastic step was the failure of the Democrats in Congress to cut off funding for the war. She also faulted Pelosi for not signing on to introduce a resolution to impeach Bush. Is this a good move for Cindy? We shall see.

Chapter 20

Have We Accomplished Anything?

I'll keep on keeping on
On until I drop
I'll keep on keeping on
I'm not ever gonna stop
   —from the song "I'll Keep on Keeping On"

What Happened to Ali?

RIGHT BEFORE TURNING IN THE FIRST DRAFT of this manuscript, I was mulling over how to end it when I happened to turn on *60 Minutes*, a program I seldom watch. I guess it was pure happenstance that I tuned it in, and although I'm the last person to put any stock in such concepts as fate and the supernatural, I have to admit that the timing was uncanny.

The segment that I caught was about Ali, the 12-year-old Iraqi boy who had lost his arms and been burned horribly and, moreover, whose entire nuclear family had perished as a result of our bombing Baghdad. As I explained in the very first paragraph of chapter 1, I had seen the heartbreaking picture of this gravely wounded boy in his hospital bed, not expected to live, in *Time* magazine in 2003, and had been motivated by it to form Grandmothers Against the War.

The *60 Minutes* story showed that Ali, now 16, had grown to be a charming, smiling schoolboy currently living in England. Though armless and reluctant to wear prostheses, Ali has become a fine painter, utilizing his feet to manipulate the brushes. Miraculously, he has written and illustrated a children's book. He returns every summer to visit his few remaining cousins and an uncle in Iraq. He participates in games and sports and is popular among his classmates. He speaks flawless English. When asked if he thinks of himself as an English person now, he replies that he still prefers to think of himself as an Iraqi.

I felt tremendous joy at seeing Ali strong and enjoying his life, seemingly a well-adjusted young man with a promising future, although I'm sure there are hidden deep scars in his psyche that can never be eradicated. I responded to this boy's painful story in as positive and constructive a way as I could by organizing the Grannies. I had always wondered what had happened to him. As I complete my book and, by chance, learn of his recovery I have a sense of coming around almost full circle. I am, however, still awaiting the only acceptable closure of this tragedy, the withdrawal of American forces from the land we desecrated.

By May 2007, most of America had come around to the belief that first motivated us Grannies back at the beginning of the war—that it was a catastrophic mistake and should be ended. I believe this indicates that we have partly achieved our goals—though the main objective of stopping the war has unfortunately not been reached as yet. Every day, practically, I hear of groups of people sitting in at congressional offices and sometimes getting arrested and even going to jail. Whereas once we were considered outrageous in our push against the tide to wake up America to the sheer wrongheadedness and tragic waste of our invasion and occupation of Iraq, now "everybody's doing it." We couldn't be more pleased.

> *"You have to ask for what you want. You may not get it all the time but if you don't ask you will never get it."*
>
> —Arlene Ellner

Grandmothers Against the War, along with our sister group, the Granny Peace Brigade, is evolving, merging into the many actions with other organizations—with Code Pink in their marvelously bold demonstrations, with United for Peace and Justice in their giant marches, with Peace Action in their frequent campaigns, among so many other creative protests occurring daily throughout the United States. Once in January and again in March of 2007, some of our members went to protest in Washington with Code Pink, where they participated in huge banner droppings on the facade of the Capitol Building. On the second occasion, the Impeachment Amendment to the Constitution was spelled out on the giant banner. Some of the Grannies united with other groups on Mother's Day to march through the Upper West Side of Manhattan, literally drumming for peace. A group of more than fifty men and women gathered at Columbus Circle to re-create Julia Ward Howe's 1870 Mothers Day for Peace Declaration. The little troupe performed on the steps of Lincoln Center, meandered through flea markets chanting, "Mother's day . . . no more war . . . Mothers say, 'Troops Home Now'!" They greeted festive brunchers at cafés on Amsterdam Avenue, strutted outside the Natural History Museum, snaked through Central Park (wheelchairs and all) and, finally, arrayed themselves in a chorus line in front of the steps of the Metropolitan Museum.

More actions in conjunction with other peace groups have

included a really good new one, the Phone-a-Thon, where we set up in a central place with a table and chairs and bring our cell phones and encourage passersby to use them free of charge to call their representatives to demand that they stop funding the war. I was incredibly encouraged to see so many young people at a Phone-a-Thon recently. I understand the Bay Area Grandmothers Against the War in San Francisco are going to institute a similar event, and our Dr. Pat Salamon has started one in her Maryland area.

However, we do still try to come up with creative actions on our own and get noticed by the press and media. We want to keep the concept of grandmother opposition to the war before the public, because we feel it has a special ability to inspire. We've kept on keeping on. In that spirit, on July 4, 2007, the Grannies and Norman Siegel read parts of the Constitution and Declaration of Independence aloud in Strawberry Fields, the lovely little oasis in Central Park created by Yoko Ono in memory of her husband, John Lennon. We also recently held our first teach-in. The subject under discussion was the need to close United States military bases abroad. Among the many items of information the audience was given was that there are more than seven hundred such installations in every continent except Antartica, and many more in the planning stages.

So, what have we accomplished, if anything? There is no way to measure our effect in helping the antiwar movement to evolve. But we were out there in the streets practically from the beginning of the conflict, when it was considered unpatriotic by some to protest the war. Some accused us of being traitors, of hurting our troops. But we stuck it out. I believe, and so do the other Grannies, that we were part of the vanguard that, bit by bit, converted the public from a small minority of war opponents into what is now the majority. We like to think we sent out vibrations that were received in invisible ways. In at least one instance we know of, one of the many photos of the Granny vigil snapped by a tourist from Japan found its way back to friends and family there, and one of them launched her own antiwar vigil in Tokyo. Hopefully, we've inspired others, too. Maybe somebody in Billings, Montana, saw our story in his or her local newspaper and wrote a letter to a congressman. Possibly, a teenage boy walked by us at Rockefeller Center and heard one of our Vets for Peace tell him, "Don't sign up," and urged his parents to fill out the Opt-Out form we gave him, so the recruiters couldn't get his home telephone number.

Among the accomplishments we may be able to claim is penetration of the media. When we began our activities, there wasn't much in newspapers or on television about any antiwar undertakings. Remember how the media practically beat the drum for the invasion of Iraq? Remember "embedded"? Remember the newscasters' almost gleeful cackling as they blithely transmitted to the world our "Shock and Awe" bombing of Baghdad, as if they were presenting the latest sitcom?

We broke through the wall, so to speak, perhaps simply by virtue of the novelty of grandmothers going out to the streets to not only protest but be arrested and jailed. This seemed to appeal to journalists sufficiently that they were able to overlook whatever strictures the networks or newspaper publishers may have imposed on them regarding reporting about citizens' rising up against the administration's grossly unconscionable attack on Iraq.

I think, also, we were able to dispel a bit the feeling of people in other countries, that all Americans were Bush boobs thirsting for blood in other people's lands. We achieved this partly by doing our weekly vigil in one of New York's most popular tourist meccas, so foreign visitors by the hundreds every week had (and still have) visible proof that there is indeed an opposition. We also were able to ameliorate this negative impression through the foreign documentaries made about us, and worldwide news coverage of our arrest and trial. Demonstrating that some Americans fought against the war became even more palpable on our two visits to Germany. This is not a small achievement. In view of the fact that the United States is now looked on with great disfavor by most of the world, I think that even the small scale of foreign persons we encountered and persuaded that many Americans have a conscience and an awareness of the evils our government has foisted on Iraq is extremely valuable.

Judging by e-mails and letters we get through our Web sites, it appears that we can claim to have had another impact. I receive message after message from grandmothers—many in small remote parts of the country—saying they hate the war and want to join our effort. If they aren't located in or near New York, where they could join our activities directly, I refer them to a wonderful lady, Lorraine Krofchok, president of Grandmothers for Peace International, who either points them to a local chapter of her organization or tells them how to establish their own.

Grandmothers for Peace is a worldwide organization. They have been in existence much longer than my little clump of grannies. They have tackled many issues—nuclear disarmament, closing the School of the Americas, and, of course, ending the occupation of Iraq. Lorraine has been a huge help to me, instructing and encouraging me all along the way. She lives in Elk Grove, California, and I occasionally think of our efforts as the two of us holding the country together from both ends. Well, if one man can destroy the whole world, two women can figuratively keep a country in one piece. Although Lorraine hasn't gotten the kind of international coverage we got when we were "busted" at Times Square, she has done ten times more in terms of fighting against the industrial-military establishment and the Bush administration, and is, to my mind, one of the most important unsung heroes we have.

No, we can't measure our impact. We can't count the numbers of people we've influenced. But, we do see the changes in the attitudes of the public toward this monstrous war and see clearly that they want it ended, and maybe, just maybe, we had something to do with that change.

At a recent vigil, after I had mostly completed this book, one of the Grannies pointed out to me another positive result of our actions, something I hadn't thought of. She said that the vigil provided her with a very necessary outlet via which to vent her frustration and anger about the war and a way for her to feel that she was able to do something about it. I realized that she was right. I, too, have attained a much-needed means, through my antiwar activities, to express feelings that I wouldn't have been able to bear otherwise. And, win or lose, at least I can never berate myself for not having tried. But our job isn't over. Now, as much as ever, we must keep the pressure on. Congress is slowly coming around on the Iraq issue but they are very shaky and dragging their feet. They need to be reminded over and over again that we expect them to put a stop to this tragedy. Thus, my vigil continues and will continue until the troops are brought home. The Granny Peace Brigade meets weekly to plan legislative action and keeps on protesting, marching, and implementing new ventures on behalf of peace. In the words of my song:

> *Grannies, let's unite*
> *While we are still upright*
> *Let's protest that parasite*
> *Watch out! we've just begun to fight*
> *We've . . . just . . . begun . . . to . . . fight!*

Index